THE ONE BIG BOOK

GRADE 6

For English, Math, and Science

- ★ Includes Math, English, Science - all in one book
- ★ Detailed instructions to teach and learn with pictures and examples
- ★ Best book for home schooling, practicing, and teaching
- ★ Includes answers with detailed explanations

Detailed instructions along with interesting activities

www.aceacademicpublishing.com

Author: Ace Academic Publishing

Prepaze is a sister company of Ace Academic Publishing. Intrigued by the unending possibilities of the internet and its role in education, Prepaze was created to spread the knowledge and learning across all corners of the world through an online platform. We equip ourselves with state-of-the-art technologies so that knowledge reaches the students through the quickest and the most effective channels.

The materials for our books are written by award winning teachers with several years of teaching experience. All our books are aligned with the state standards and are widely used by many schools throughout the country.

For enquiries and bulk order, contact us at the following address:

3736, Fallon Road, #403
Dublin, CA 94568
www.aceacademicpublishing.com

Ace Academic Publishing
ACHIEVING EXCELLENCE TOGETHER

This book contains copyright material. The purchase of this material entitles the buyer to use this material for personal and classroom use only. Reproducing the content for commercial use is strictly prohibited. Contact us to learn about options to use it for an entire school district or other commercial use.

ISBN: 978-1-949383-49-2
© Ace Academic Publishing, 2022

Other books from Ace Academic Publishing

 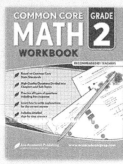 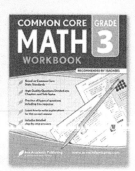 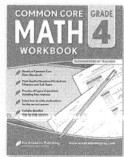 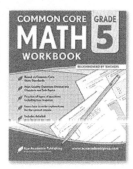

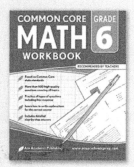 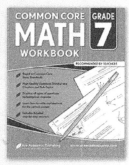 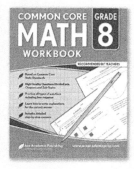  

Ace Academic Publishing
ACHIEVING EXCELLENCE TOGETHER

Other books from Ace Academic Publishing

 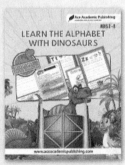   

Ace Academic Publishing
ACHIEVING EXCELLENCE TOGETHER

CONTENTS

ENGLISH

Language	**2**
Pronoun Case	2
Intensive Pronouns	6
Shift in Pronoun	8
Vague Pronoun	10
Punctuation	13
Spelling	16
Sentence Pattern	22
Context Clues	27
Affixes and Roots	29
Reference Materials	31
Simile and Metaphor	34
Personification and Hyperbole	41
Word Analogies	43
Connotation and Denotation	46

Reading:	
Informational Text	**70**
The Founding Fathers of the USA	70
Pet Survey	75

Reading: Literature	**49**
The Beetle	49
Pirate Story	61
The Moon	65

Writing	**78**
Writing Process	78
Argumentative Writing	82
Explanatory Writing	85
Narrative Writing	87
Research Writing	89

www.prepaze.com

prepaze

MATH

Ratio and Proportional Relationships — 92
- Fruit Bowl Ratio — 93
- Fun Project at Lego Corp — 94
- How Many Stars and Moons? — 95
- How Long Will Miss. Snail Crawl? — 96
- How Much Flour? — 98
- Trip to the Farm — 104
- Tom's Math Test — 105

Number System — 106
- Kiara's Kitchen — 106
- Help Ryan Floor the Pool — 107
- Traffic Light Mystery — 108
- Product Rule for HCF and LCM — 109
- Which Is the Best Buy? — 110
- Mark the Temperatures — 113

Expressions and Equations — 115
- Solve the Inequalities — 116
- Determine the Solution — 117
- Hanger Problem — 118
- What Is the Inequality? — 119
- Create Number Sentences — 119
- True or False — 120
- Can Richard Play in the Ball Pit? — 120
- Word Problems — 121
- Evaluate for x, y — 123
- Riddle Time — 127
- Story Problems — 128
- Angles at the Parking Lot — 131
- Determine the Tiles to Fit the Corner — 134
- Posters and Fliers — 135
- Noah's Saving Plan — 137
- Complete the Table — 139
- Area and Perimeter — 140
- Is Ron Right? — 142

Geometry — 143
- Drek's Swimming Pool — 146
- Lucy's Kitchen Counter — 148
- Area of a School — 150
- An Aquarium Math Problem — 153
- Football Ground Math Problem — 155
- A Juicy Problem — 158
- Help Jessica Make Gift Boxes — 160

Statistics and Probability — 161
- Categorical or Numerical Data Sets — 161
- Lunch Hour at Big Burgers — 162
- Kyle's Christmas Tree — 164
- A Science Experiment — 166
- What's Your Favorite Flavor? — 167
- How Many Pets Does Noah's Friends Have? — 170

www.prepaze.com

prepaze

SCIENCE

Earth Sciences - Plate Tectonics and Earth's Structure — 176

Tectonic Plates	176
Crossword	178
Causes and Effects of Plate Boundaries	179
Tectonic Plates Around the World	180
Research on Natural Disasters	182
Layers of the Earth	185
Faults and Earthquakes	187
Analyze an Earthquake	188

Earth Sciences - Shaping Earth's Surface — 191

Factors That Shape the Earth	191
Shaping the Surface of the Earth	192
Journey through the Meander	194
Types of Rocks	196
Crossword Time	197
Journey in a Lahar	199
Create a Report	201

Earth Sciences - Energy in the Earth System — 203

Sun - Major Source of Energy for Weather	203
Ocean Currents	203
Greenhouse Effect	206
Climate vs Weather	207
Convection in the Mantle	210

www.prepaze.com

prepaze

Physical Sciences	212
Heat Energy and Heat Transfer	212
Heat Transfer	212
Testing Heat Transfer	213
Activity for Heat Transfer	214
Heat Transfer through Materials	216
Modes of Heat Transfer	217

Life Sciences - Ecology	218
Energy Flow in Living Things	218
Ecosystem and Its Factors	219
Producers and Consumers	223
Food Chains and Food Webs	224
Energy Flow in Food Webs	226
Relationships Between Organisms	228
Animals and Adaptations	232
Reason behind Adaptations	233
Regions and Adaptations	235
Who am I?	236

Resources	239
Types of Resources	239
Renewable and Non-Renewable Resources	239
Compare and Contrast	241
Find the Word	242
Biomes That We Live in	243
Energy Scavenger Hunt	246
Creative Writing	248
Conservation of Natural Resources	250
Vocabulary Check	253

Answer Keys 255

English

This book enables your children to explore the English language and develop the necessary expertise. A series of thought-provoking exercises, engaging activities, and engrossing puzzles facilitate your children with understanding the intricacies of the English language.

Pronoun Case

A pronoun is a word that substitutes a noun. The personal pronouns and the interrogative pronoun "who" have three cases: subjective, objective, and possessive.

Different cases of a pronoun are used depending on the position of the pronoun in a sentence.

	Subjective	Objective	Possessive
1st Person Singular	I	me	my/mine
1st Person Plural	we	us	our/ours
2nd Person	you	you	your/yours
3rd Person Singular	he/she/it	him/her/it	his/(her/hers)/its
3rd Person Plural	they	them	their/theirs
Interrogative Pronoun	who/ whoever	whom/ whomever	whose/ whosever

Examples

They live in this house. (subject of the sentence - hence subjective case)

I saw **them** in this house. (object of the sentence - hence objective case)

This house is **theirs**. (possessive case)

Use the appropriate pronoun case of the pronouns given in the parentheses.

1. None of us is more knowledgeable than _____ .

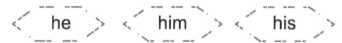
he / him / his

2. Pollution affects _____ environmentalists.

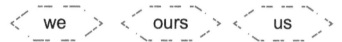
we / ours / us

3. Is he or _____ hosting the party?

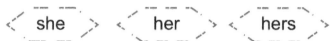
she / her / hers

4. Three of them took _____ car.

we / us / our

5. They appreciated _____ arriving on time.

you / your / yours

6. The Principal told us and _____ to contribute.

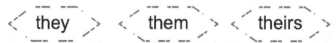
they / them / theirs

Who or Whom?

Choose the correct pronoun case.

1. _____ should I trust?

2. Is he the one for _____ the remark is intended?

3. He is the one _____ solved the riddle.

4. _____ called the parents?

5. The celebrity _____ we met was generous.

Yes or No

Write YES against the sentences with the correct pronoun case, and NO against the sentences with incorrect pronoun case.

		Yes or No
1	The protagonist in the story is she.	
2	Us students love the library.	
3	I am as brave as she.	
4	The coach gave he and she some pointers.	
5	Who should I give the notes?	
6	The misunderstanding between Lisa and I was caused by her.	
7	My sister and me went upstairs to do our homework.	
8	My father, who has a student loan, works two shifts.	

www.prepaze.com

Correct the pronoun errors in the following sentences. Write NC for sentences with No Changes.

1. He joined she at the mall.

_____

2. Jose and me were invited to the dance.

_____

3. She is smarter than me.

_____

4. Whom should I give the remote?

_____

5. I noticed that it was them who started the work.

_____

Intensive Pronouns

These pronouns are used to add emphasis to a noun or a pronoun within a sentence. The sentence usually makes sense even when these pronouns are removed.

Example

I **myself** can't imagine going there.

The pronoun **myself** is not essential here. However, it adds emphasis.

Examples of intensive pronouns:

Singular	Plural
myself	ourselves
herself/himself/itself	themselves
yourself	yourselves

Use the appropriate intensive pronoun to complete each sentence.

themselves   herself   itself
yourselves   himself   ourselves

1. He bought _____ a new car.

2. The dog _____ makes the bed after every nap.

3. Sophia _____ painted the rooms.

4. They organized the event _____ .

5. We _____ chose the subjects for our experiment.

Shift in Pronoun

This happens when a writer starts with a particular type of pronoun and suddenly shifts to another. This results in faulty sentences as they confuse the readers.

Example

Incorrect: When we choose a career path, you should carefully consider all your options.

Correct: When we choose a career path, **we** should carefully consider all **our** options.

Here, the writer has shifted from first person "we" to second person "you." This can be fixed by changing all the pronouns to either first person or second person.

Identify Pronoun Shift

Choose the underlined part of the sentence that has a pronoun shift. If no error exists, choose "No change."

1. If <u>you</u> have the will, <u>people</u> will be able to achieve <u>your goals</u>.
      A   B   C

   (A)　(B)　(C)　(No change)

2. <u>We</u> said, "<u>We</u> are happy to be here for <u>you</u>."
      A   B   C

   (A)　(B)　(C)　(No change)

3. <u>Artists</u> need to stay motivated and inspired. <u>They</u> can find the motivation within, or
      A   B

   <u>we</u> can find it outside.
   C

   (A)　(B)　(C)　(No change)

4. <u>She</u> said, "<u>I</u> am happy to help him and <u>his</u> friends."
      A   B   C

   (A)　(B)　(C)　(No change)

5. <u>They</u> said that <u>they</u> will provide accommodation for <u>us</u>.
      A   B   C

   (A)　(B)　(C)　(No change)

Vague Pronoun

When writers use pronouns such as it, which, this, or that, they can leave the readers wondering to whom or what these pronouns refer.

Example

> Her child puts little effort in learning, and now she got him a tablet. This is going to lower his grade.

Is the pronoun "this" referring to "the fact that the child does not put enough effort in learning" or "the tablet"? This can be fixed by adding a noun after "this."

Revision: Her child puts little effort in learning, and now she got him a tablet. This tablet is going to lower his grade.

Rewrite the sentences fixing the vague pronoun references.

1. Tom went to congratulate Harry after he completed work.

2. Rosa told Jenny that the principal advised her not to cut class.

3. The library and the bookshop are closing. We already miss it.

4. Mom told Christy that she would watch her favorite movie.

Spot the Error

Circle if the given statement has no pronoun errors, and

circle if the statement has a pronoun error.

#	Statement	✓	✗
1	Our parents made all the calls and organized everything ourselves.	✓	✗
2	When my mom used to work there, employees had to wear uniforms.	✓	✗
3	The project that I'm working on is different from your.	✓	✗
4	There are no secrets between Chris and I.	✓	✗
5	Elijah, Jacob, and I decided to work together.	✓	✗
6	Though Charlotte and Isabella were late, she was allowed to take the test.	✓	✗

Punctuation

A **comma** is a frequently used punctuation mark. It is used to indicate a soft pause within a sentence.

One of the uses of commas is to set off nonrestrictive clauses or parenthetical elements. **Parentheses** and **dashes** can also be used to separate parenthetical elements.

Examples

> The meeting, nevertheless, was a success.

In this sentence, the comma provides a pause and also sets off the parenthetical element "nevertheless."

> The dancers, who rehearsed for days, gave an impeccable performance.
>
> The dancers – who rehearsed for days – gave an impeccable performance.
>
> The dancers (who rehearsed for days) gave an impeccable performance.

In these sentences, commas, dashes, and parentheses are used to set off a nonrestrictive clause.

Choose Me

Identify the sentence with the correct punctuation marks.

1. a. Nathan lived in Juneau, Alaska, for 8 years.

   b. Nathan lived in Juneau Alaska, for 8 years.

   c. Nathan lived in Juneau Alaska for 8 years.

2. a. Achilles in Greek legend is the greatest warrior and fighter among the (Achaians).

   b. Achilles in (Greek legend) is the greatest warrior, and fighter among the Achaians.

   c. Achilles (in Greek legend) is the greatest warrior and fighter among the Achaians.

3. a. In 2005 Rebecca and a partner bought a small general store on credit in New Salem, Illinois.

   b. In 2005, Rebecca, and a partner, bought a small general store on credit in New Salem, Illinois.

   c. In 2005, Rebecca and a partner bought a small general store on credit in New Salem, Illinois.

4. a. William—Shakespeare—who was an English poet, playwright, and actor is known as Bard of Avon.

   b. William Shakespeare who was an English poet, playwright, and actor—is known as—Bard of Avon.

   c. William Shakespeare—who was an English poet, playwright, and actor—is known as Bard of Avon.

5. a. Threats of flooding rainfall, tornadoes and gusty winds, in my opinion will continue along the coast.

   b. Threats of flooding rainfall, tornadoes, and gusty winds, in my opinion, will continue along the coast.

   c. Threats of flooding rainfall, tornadoes, and gusty winds in my opinion, will continue along the coast.

6. a. The biggest concern as you (will see) is the parking space.

   b. The biggest (concern) as you will see is the parking space.

   c. The biggest concern (as you will see) is the parking space.

Add commas, dashes, or parentheses to fix the below sentences.

> We do not recommend that no.

> Take for example the way he runs his office; it is a testimony of his loyalty.

> The warnings however did not have an effect.

> A few people who I won't name don't appreciate what they have.

Spelling

Though English is the most commonly spoken language in the world, it can be tricky in terms of spelling.

Factors such as different ways of spelling the same sound, same spelling of words with different sound, borrowed language, odd combination of letters, or silent letters can make spelling quite challenging for learners.

Examples

The following are examples of words that are often misspelled.

| dilemma | stationery | camouflage | committed |

Word Scramble

Rearrange the letters to find the words.

R O E U S S C R P R

O P I Y R I T R

A C T R T I F A

A E L O A T E B R

R D T I A S C

T V R R I E E E

 **Untangle Me**

Follow the lines and rearrange the letters. Write the correct word in the boxes.

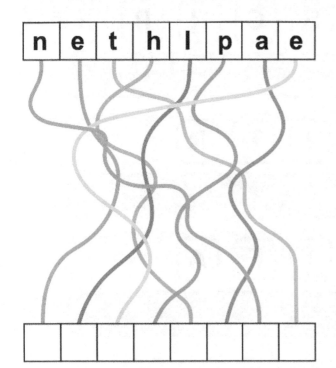

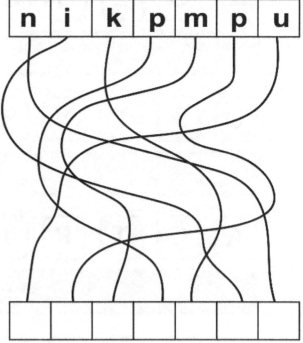

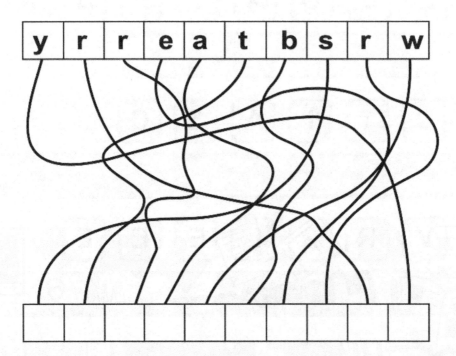

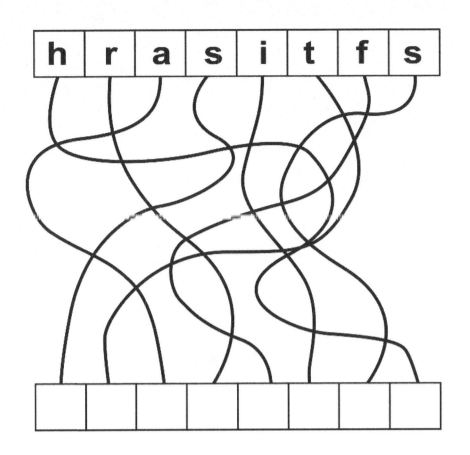
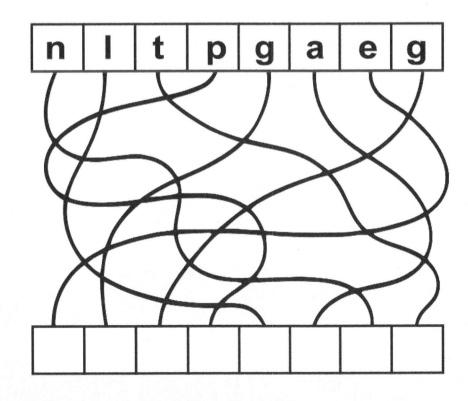

Secret Word

Figure out the secret word.

A	B	C	D	E	F	G	H	I	J	K	L	M
₪	Φ	Ꝏ	⌐	β	Δ	љ	¬	€	~	^	Ҷ	π

N	O	P	Q	R	S	T	U	V	W	X	Y	Z
Ω	∞	П	μ	Ђ	ϟ	ж	ђ	э	ψ	∫	Г	ф

Decode the below word using the table above.

Ꝏ Ђ Г П ж ∞ љ Ђ ₪ П ¬ Г

C R Y P T O G R A P H Y

Write a secret word/message for your friends.

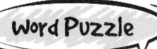

- plaster
- thermometer
- stethoscope
- pill
- mask
- syringe
- doctor
- hospital
- ambulance
- mixture
- virus

Sentence Pattern

To keep things interesting in speech and writing, we often use sentences of varied lengths and patterns.

Below are a few basic sentence patterns.

<u>I</u> <u>ran.</u> Subject Verb	S + V
<u>We</u> <u>love</u> <u>English.</u> Subject Verb Object	S + V + O
<u>We</u> <u>are</u> <u>happy.</u> Subject Verb Complement	S + V + C

Object of a sentence is the person or thing that receives the action. Each of the below sentences has a subject followed by a verb. Use the appropriate **object** to complete each sentence.

1. We played _____.

2. They ordered a _____.

3. Josh entered the _____.

4. The worm crawled into a _____.

5. My brother made the _____.

Identify the sentence pattern and match accordingly.

Sentence	Pattern
I met them.	V+O
It rained today.	S+V+IO+DO
This makes me happy.	S+V+C
The nurse gave her an injection.	S+V+O
Call him.	S+V+A
They seem anxious.	S+V+O+C

Jumbled Sentences

Arrange the parts of the sentences following the sentence pattern given. Begin the sentences with capital letters and end them with appropriate punctuation marks.

1. S+V+C — a mechanic / is / her father

2. A+S+V — they / yesterday / ran

3. S+V+O+C — got / pierced / he / his ears

4. S+V+IO+DO — us / their car / sold / they

5. S+V+O — I / a poem / wrote

6. S+V+O+C+A — lost / his wallet / Jose / in the subway / with his license

This or That?

Choose the pattern of the given sentences.

1. My mother gave me a present.
   - ☐ S+V+IO+DO
   - ☐ S+V+O+C+A

2. She sent a postcard from Rome.
   - ☐ S+V+IO+DO
   - ☐ S+V+O+A

3. You seem upset today.
   - ☐ S+V+O+A
   - ☐ S+V+C+A

4. My uncle's friend raised a wild animal.
   - ☐ S+V+O
   - ☐ S+V+C

5. I took my pet, wounded to the vet.
   - ☐ S+V+O+C+A
   - ☐ S+V+C+A

Identify the Pattern

Read the sentences and write the pattern in the given boxes.

1. Excuse me. ⬚

2. It is dirty here. ⬚

3. They sold the house last year. ⬚

4. The children were tired. ⬚

Context Clues

Often we come across words for which we don't know the meaning. Most of the time, writers leave clues within a sentence or in the surrounding text to help us understand difficult or technical words.

Example

> She thought her friend would be **distraught** on hearing the news of her son's accident.

The above sentence has an unfamiliar word, but there aren't enough clues to guess the meaning. Look at the sentence below:

> She thought her friend would be **distraught** on hearing the news of her son's accident, **but she remained calm.**

In the above sentence, the use of "but" in the context clarifies that distraught is the opposite of "calm." With that, we can conclude that distraught means distressed or upset.

What Is the Meaning?

Find the meaning of the underlined words using the clues.

1. Gabriella has many friends because she is a <u>gregarious</u> person.

    a. friendly

    b. introverted

    c. naïve

2. The thought of harming any animal is <u>abhorrent</u> and painful to most people.

    a. admirable

    b. commendable

    c. disgusting

3. Since the journey was too <u>arduous</u>, we made multiple stops to rest and refresh.

    a. effortless

    b. tiring

    c. condescending

4. The speech I downloaded was almost <u>inaudible</u>; I had to play it on a speaker to hear it clearly.

    a. advisable

    b. perishable

    c. unhearable

5. The enemies had to <u>capitulate</u> to our attack as they realized they were surrounded and could not win.

    a. resist

    b. surrender

    c. benevolent

www.prepaze.com

Affixes and Roots

Affixes are letters added before or after a root or base word to change its meaning or function.

Example

Roots: nav al

a morph ous

Prefixes: pre determine

re unite

Suffixes: move ment

planet ary

Add Prefixes

For the following words, add the appropriate prefixes to form their opposites.

understand	
connect	
interpret	
close	
behave	
agree	
acceptable	
engage	

Match the words with the appropriate suffixes.

conform	ness
manage	ing
run	ful
defense	able
wish	ist
aware	ible

Reference Materials

Reference materials are used for research, to study, or to check facts. There are reliable and easily accessible reference materials such as encyclopedia, dictionary, thesaurus, and maps.

Examples

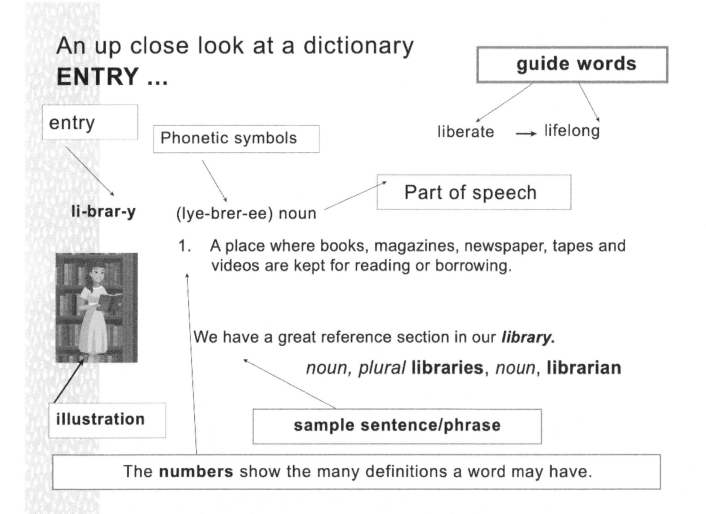

Use a Dictionary

Find the meaning of the following words and use them in a sentence.

1. **disparage**

   Meaning:

   Sentence:

2. **galvanizing**

   Meaning:

   Sentence:

3. **ramify**

   Meaning:

   Sentence:

4. **adversarial**

   Meaning:

   Sentence:

5. **undulate**

   Meaning:

   Sentence:

6. **deliberate**

   Meaning:

   Sentence:

Use a Thesaurus

Find the various synonyms for the following words.

aggravate	sporadic

accolade	embezzle

erratic	retrograde

Simile and Metaphor

A simile compares two things using the words "like" or "as."

> **This scarf is as light as a feather.**
>
> The simile here shows how the **scarf** weighs light as a **feather**.

Circle 🙂 if the given statement has a simile, and circle 😐 if the statement does not have a simile.

This dress fits like a glove.	🙂	😐
The room is exactly as she described.	🙂	😐
She is brave as a lion.	🙂	😐
My siblings fight like cats and dogs.	🙂	😐
He missed the beginning as he was late.	🙂	😐
They looked as if they were lost.	🙂	😐
The horse ran like the wind.	🙂	😐

Construct Similes

Use LIKE or AS to connect the given words. The words are not given in any particular order. Match the words to make similes, and write them in the space given below.

How to do it:

1st thing + quality + as/like + 2nd thing

My cousin | swims | like | a fish.
1st thing + quality + as/like + 2nd thing

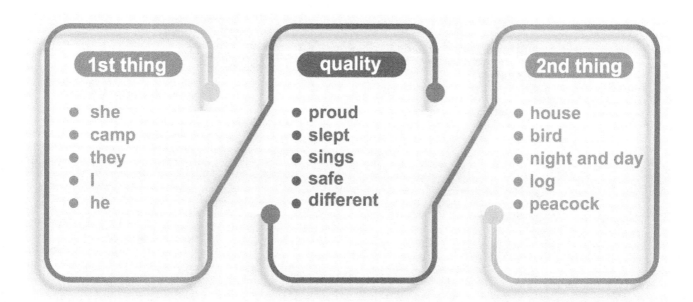

1st thing
- she
- camp
- they
- I
- he

quality
- proud
- slept
- sings
- safe
- different

2nd thing
- house
- bird
- night and day
- log
- peacock

Metaphor

A metaphor compares two things without using the words "like" or "as."

You are my sunshine!

The metaphor here directly compares someone to sunshine instead of using any specific attribute of sunshine.

This metaphor could mean that the person is the light of someone's life, special, or important.

Write YES for sentences with metaphors and NO for sentences without a metaphor.

		Yes or No
1	They are guarding the house.	
2	Ashley is an angel.	
3	My parents believe me.	
4	He is my biggest admirer.	
5	She is a tiger.	
6	Eden is a teacher.	
7	Ann broke into the conversation.	

What Is the Quality?

Find the quality that is compared in these metaphors. Explain the comparison in the space provided.

This place is an oven.

Explain: _____

Children flocked to see the show.

Explain: _____

She is a star.

Explain: _____

Lee is an early bird.

Explain: _____

The world is a stage.

Explain: _____

Categorize the below statements. Write the serial numbers in the respective circle.

Serial No.	Statements
1	The child is afraid of darkness.
2	They are watching us like a hawk.
3	She watched as the train left.
4	The relationship turned sour.
5	The bannister is as cold as ice.
6	Books are better than movies.
7	My brother is a rock.
8	The kettle was as black as coal.

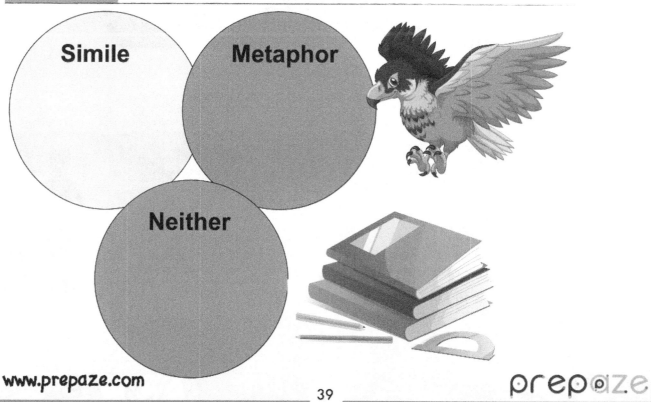

Write Metaphors

Think creatively and write 4 metaphors. Remember not to use the words "as" or "like."

01

02

03

04

Riddle

What is a 5-letter word that has the same pronunciation even if the last 4 letters are removed?

Personification and Hyperbole

Personification is a figurative language used to give human qualities to inanimate objects.

Example

The dying plants were begging for water.

A plant cannot beg or cry, but these human qualities are added for effect.

Hyperbole is a figurative language used to add exaggeration for emphasis or humor.

Example

Stephanie can run faster than a cheetah.

It is not humanly possible to outrun a cheetah, but the speed is exaggerated here to add emphasis.

Personification or Hyperbole?

Read the sentences and choose the correct answer.

1. The leaves danced in the wind.

   Personification   **Hyperbole**

2. My backpack weighs a ton.

   Personification   **Hyperbole**

3. I have reminded my team a million times to proofread their work.

   Personification   **Hyperbole**

4. New York is a city that never sleeps.

   Personification   **Hyperbole**

5. I love you to the moon and back.

   Personification   **Hyperbole**

6. We watched as the angry storm devoured the garden.

   Personification   **Hyperbole**

Word Analogies

Analogy shows a relationship between words, and aides in vocabulary building. There are different types of analogies.

Example

brush : paint

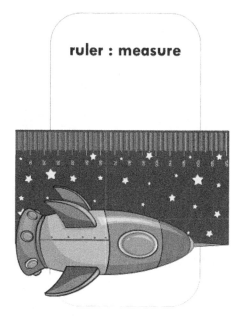

ruler : measure

In this example, the word pair on the left and the word pair on the right share the same relationship. The relationship is "object to function." The object "brush" helps us "paint" just like the object "ruler" helps us "measure."

Below are a few analogy types with examples:

Part to whole	page : book
Cause and effect	fire : burn
Antonym	exterior : interior

Complete the Analogy

Find the relationship between the first pair of words. Then complete the second pair using the same relationship.

1. grass : green :: sapphire : _____
   a. blue
   b. yellow
   c. green
   d. brown

2. tired : exhausted :: seize : _____
   a. determine
   b. reproach
   c. insincere
   d. confiscate

3. anchor : ship :: glass : _____
   a. shatter
   b. clear
   c. window
   d. knot

4. banana : peel :: candy : _____
   a. protect
   b. wrapper
   c. sugar
   d. sweetness

5. imbecile : genius :: conserve : _____
   a. disguise
   b. preserve
   c. squander
   d. economise

Find the Relationship

Select the choice that best describes the relationship between the word pairs.

1. beaver : rodent :: shirt : clothing

    a) part to whole

    b) object to classification

    c) performer to action

    d) part to part

2. microscope : magnify :: lighthouse : warn

    a) object to location

    b) object to classification

    c) problem to solution

    d) object to function

3. sector : circle :: entry : dictionary

    a) performer to action

    b) object to group

    c) part to whole

    d) part to part

4. teacher : educate :: author : write

    a) part to whole

    b) object to function

    c) object to group

    d) performer to action

Connotation and Denotation

A few synonyms though share the same meaning, have positive or negative feelings associated with them. This is called connotation.

The words that are used with primary meaning without any positive or negative association is called denotation or neutral meaning.

This looks different.

This looks peculiar.

This is unique.

Here, the words different, unique, and peculiar are synonymous.

However, the word **unique** (appealing in an interesting way) has a **positive connotation**, and the word **peculiar** (which could mean weird) has a **negative connotation**. The word **different** is neutral.

Neutral, Positive, or Negative?

Identify the connotation of the underlined words.

1. She has a very <u>immature</u> sense of humor.

    Neutral   Positive   Negative

2. The <u>slender</u> man who walked in seems to get a lot of attention.

    Neutral   Positive   Negative

3. The lay off has made her <u>egotistical</u> and insecure.

    Neutral   Positive   Negative

4. Keeping my voice <u>conversational</u>, I continued to enquire about the airport.

    Neutral   Positive   Negative

5. We remained <u>steadfast</u> in our determination to reach our goals.

    Neutral   Positive   Negative

Complete the fish

Write the positive words from the list on the upper side of the fishbone and write the synonymous negative words on the other side.

hyperactive   energetic   aroma
stench   assertive   pushy

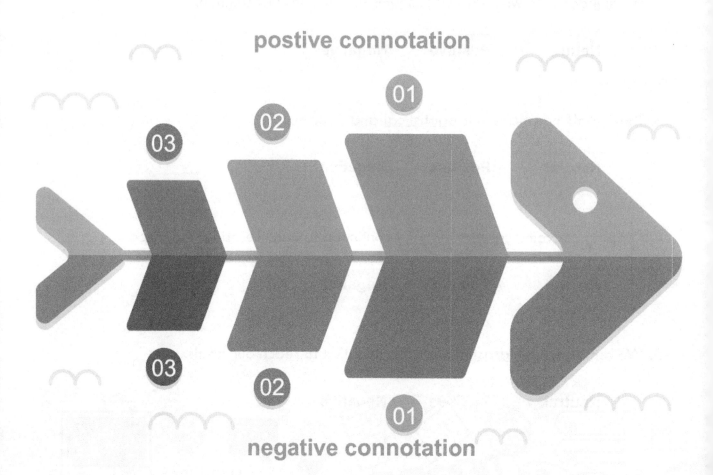

Reading: Literature

The emperor's favourite horse was shod with gold. It had a golden shoe on each of its feet.

And why was this?

He was a beautiful creature, with delicate legs, bright intelligent eyes, and a mane that hung down over his neck like a veil. He had carried his master through the fire and smoke of battle, and heard the bullets whistling around him, had kicked, bitten, and taken part in the fight when the enemy advanced, and had sprung with his master on his back over the fallen foe, and had saved the crown of red gold, and the life of the emperor, which was more valuable than the red gold; and that is why the emperor's horse had golden shoes.

And a beetle came creeping forth.

"First the great ones," said he, "and then the little ones; but greatness is not the only thing that does it." And so saying, he stretched out his thin legs.

"And pray what do you want?" asked the smith.

"Golden shoes, to be sure," replied the beetle.

"Why, you must be out of your senses," cried the smith. "Do you want to have golden shoes too?"

"Golden shoes? certainly," replied the beetle. "Am I not just as good as that big creature yonder, that is waited on, and brushed, and has meat and drink put before him? Don't I belong to the imperial stable?"

---
* By Hans Christian Andersen

"But why is the horse to have golden shoes? Don't you understand that?" asked the smith.

"Understand? I understand that it is a personal slight offered to myself," cried the beetle. "It is done to annoy me, and therefore I am going into the world to seek my fortune."

"Go along!" said the smith.

"You're a rude fellow!" cried the beetle; and then he went out of the stable, flew a little way, and soon afterwards found himself in a beautiful flower garden, all fragrant with roses and lavender.

"Is it not beautiful here?" asked one of the little lady-birds that flew about, with their delicate wings and their red-and-black shields on their backs. "How sweet it is here—how beautiful it is!"

"I'm accustomed to better things," said the beetle. "Do you call this beautiful? Why, there is not so much as a dung-heap."

Then he went on, under the shadow of a great stack, and found a caterpillar crawling along.

"How beautiful the world is!" said the caterpillar : "the sun is so warm, and everything so enjoyable! And when I go to sleep, and die, as they call it, I shall wake up as a butterfly, with beautiful wings to fly with."

"How conceited you are!" exclaimed the stag-beetle. "Fly about as a butterfly, indeed! I've come out of the stable of the emperor, and no one there, not even the emperor's favourite horse—that by the way wears my cast-off golden shoes—has any such idea. To have wings to fly! why, we can fly now;" and he spread his wings and flew away. "I don't want to be annoyed, and yet I am annoyed," he said, as he flew off.

Soon afterwards he fell down upon a great lawn. For awhile he lay there and feigned slumber; at last he fell asleep in earnest.

Suddenly a heavy shower of rain came falling from the clouds. The beetle woke up at the noise, and wanted to escape into the earth, but could not. He was tumbled over and over; sometimes he was swimming on his stomach, sometimes on his back, and as for flying, that was out of the question; he doubted whether he should escape from the place with his life. He therefore remained lying where he was.

When the weather had moderated a little, and the beetle had rubbed the water out of his eyes, he saw something gleaming. It was linen that had been placed there to bleach. He managed to make his way up to it, and crept into a fold of the damp linen. Certainly the place was not so comfortable to lie in as the warm stable; but there was no better to be had, and therefore he remained lying there for a whole day and a whole night, and the rain kept on during all the time. Towards morning he crept forth: he was very much out of temper about the climate.

On the linen two frogs were sitting. Their bright eyes absolutely gleamed with pleasure.

"Wonderful weather this!" one of them cried. "How refreshing!

And the linen keeps the water together so beautifully. My hind legs seem to quiver as if I were going to swim."

"I should like to know," said the second, "if the swallow, who flies so far round, in her many journeys in foreign lands ever meets with a better climate than this. What delicious dampness! It is really as if one were lying in a wet ditch. Whoever does not rejoice in this, certainly does not love his fatherland."

"Have you been in the emperor's stable?" asked the beetle: "there the dampness is warm and refreshing. That's the climate for me; but I cannot take it with me on my journey. Is there never a muck-heap, here in the garden, where a person of rank, like myself, can feel himself at home, and take up his quarters?"

But the frogs either did not or would not understand him.

"I never ask a question twice!" said the beetle, after he had already asked this one three times without receiving any answer.

Then he went a little farther, and stumbled against a fragment of pottery, that certainly ought not to have been lying there; but as it was once there, it gave a good shelter against wind and weather. Here dwelt several families of earwigs; and these did not require much, only sociality. The female members of the community were full of the purest maternal affection, and accordingly each one considered her own child the most beautiful and cleverest of all.

"Our son has engaged himself," said one mother. "Dear, innocent boy! His greatest hope is that he may creep one day into a clergyman's ear. It's very artless and loveable, that; and being engaged will keep him steady. What joy for a mother!"

"Our son," said another mother, "had scarcely crept out of the egg, when he was already off on his travels. He's all life and spirits; he'll run his horns off! What joy that is for a mother! Is it not so, Mr. Beetle?" for she knew the stranger by his horny coat.

"You are both quite right," said he; so they begged him to walk in; that is to say, to come as far as he could under the bit of pottery.

"Now, you also see my little earwig," observed a third mother and a fourth; "they are lovely little things, and highly amusing. They are never ill-behaved, except when they are uncomfortable in their inside; but, unfortunately, one is very subject to that at their age."

Thus each mother spoke of her baby; and the babies talked among themselves, and made use of the little nippers they have in their tails to nip the beard of the beetle.

"Yes, they are always busy about something, the little rogues!" said the mothers; and they quite beamed with maternal pride; but the beetle felt bored by that, and therefore he inquired how far it was to the nearest muck-heap.

"That is quite out in the big world, on the other side of the ditch," answered an earwig. "I hope none of my children will go so far, for it would be the death of me."

"But I shall try to get so far," said the beetle; and he went off without taking formal leave; for that is considered the polite thing to do. And by the ditch he met several friends; beetles, all of them.

"Here we live," they said. "We are very comfortable here. Might we ask you to step down into this rich mud? You must be fatigued after your journey."

"Certainly," replied the beetle. "I have been exposed to the rain, and have had to lie upon linen, and cleanliness is a thing that greatly exhausts me. I have also pains in one of my wings, from standing in a draught under a fragment of pottery. It is really quite refreshing to be among one's companions once more."

"Perhaps you come from some muck-heap?" observed the oldest of them.

"Indeed, I come from a much higher place," replied the beetle. "I came from the emperor's stable, where I was born with golden shoes on my feet. I am travelling on a secret embassy. You must not ask me any questions, for I can't betray my secret."

With this the beetle stepped down into the rich mud. There sat three young maiden beetles; and they tittered, because they did not know what to say.

"Not one of them is engaged yet," said their mother; and the beetle maidens tittered again, this time from embarrassment.

"I have never seen greater beauties in the royal stables," exclaimed the beetle, who was now resting himself.

"Don't spoil my girls," said the mother; "and don't talk to them, please, unless you have serious intentions. But of course your intentions are serious, and therefore I give you my blessing."

"Hurrah!" cried all the other beetles together; and our friend was engaged. Immediately after the betrothal came the marriage, for there was no reason for delay.

The following day passed very pleasantly, and the next in tolerable comfort; but on the third it was time to think of food for the wife, and perhaps also for children.

"I have allowed myself to be taken in," said our beetle to himself. "And now there's nothing for it but to take them in, in turn."

So said, so done. Away he went, and he stayed away all day, and stayed away all night; and his wife sat there, a forsaken widow.

"Oh," said the other beetles, "this fellow whom we received into our family is nothing more than a thorough vagabond. He has gone away, and has left his wife a burden upon our hands."

"Well, then, she shall be unmarried again, and sit here among my daughters," said the mother. "Fie on the villain who forsook her!"

In the meantime the beetle had been journeying on, and had sailed across the ditch on a cabbage leaf. In the morning two persons came to the ditch. When they saw him, they took him up, and turned him over and over, and looked very learned, especially one of them—a boy.

"Allah sees the black beetle in the black stone and in the black rock. Is not that written in the Koran?" Then he translated the beetle's name into Latin, and enlarged upon the creature's nature and history. The second person, an older scholar, voted for carrying him home. He said they wanted just such good specimens; and this seemed an uncivil speech to our beetle, and in consequence he flew suddenly out of the speaker's hand. As he had now dry wings, he flew a tolerable distance, and reached a hot-bed, where a sash of the glass roof was partly open, so he quietly slipped in and buried himself in the warm earth.

"Very comfortable it is here," said he.

Soon after he went to sleep, and dreamed that the emperor's favourite horse had fallen, and had given him his golden shoes, with the promise that he should have two more.

That was all very charming. When the beetle woke up, he crept forth and looked around him. What splendour was in the hothouse! In the background great palm trees growing up on high; the sun made them look transparent; and beneath them what a luxuriance of green, and of beaming flowers, red as fire, yellow as amber, or white as fresh-fallen snow.

"This is an incomparable plenty of plants," cried the beetle. "How good they will taste when they are decayed! A capital store-room this! There must certainly be relations of mine living here. I will just see if I can find any one with whom I may associate. I'm proud, certainly, and I'm proud of being so." And so he prowled about in the earth, and thought what a pleasant dream that was about the dying horse, and the golden shoes he had inherited.

Suddenly a hand seized the beetle, and pressed him, and turned him round and round.

The gardener's little son and a companion had come to the hot-bed, had espied the beetle, and wanted to have their fun with him. First he was wrapped in a vine leaf, and then put into warm trousers-pocket. He cribbled and crabbled about there with all his might; but he got a good pressing from the boy's hand for this, which served as a hint to him to keep quiet. Then the boy went rapidly towards the great lake that lay at the end of the garden. Here the beetle was put in an old broken wooden shoe, on which a little stick was placed upright for a mast, and to this mast the beetle was bound with a woollen thread. Now he was a sailor, and had to sail away.

The lake was not very large, but to the beetle it seemed an ocean; and he was so astonished at its extent, that he fell over on his back and kicked out with his legs.

The little ship sailed away. The current of the water seized it; but whenever it went too far from the shore, one of the boys turned up his trousers and went in after it, and brought it back to the land. But at length, just as it went merrily out again, the two boys were called away, and very harshly, so that they hurried to obey the summons, ran away from the lake, and left the little ship to its fate. Thus it drove away from the shore, farther and farther into the open sea: it was terrible work for the beetle, for he could not get away in consequence of being bound to the mast.

Then a fly came and paid him a visit.

"What beautiful weather!" said the fly. "I'll rest here, and sun myself. You have an agreeable time of it."

"You speak without knowing the facts," replied the beetle. "Don't you see that I'm a prisoner?"

"Ah! but I'm not a prisoner," observed the fly; and he flew away accordingly.

"Well, now I know the world," said the beetle to himself. "It is an abominable world. I'm the only honest person in it. First, they refuse me my golden shoes; then I have to lie on wet linen, and to stand in the draught; and, to crown all, they fasten a wife upon me. Then, when I've taken a quick step out into the world, and found out how one can have it there, and how I wished to have it, one of those human boys comes and ties me up, and leaves me to the mercy of the wild waves, while the emperor's favourite horse prances about proudly in golden shoes. That is what annoys me more than all. But one must not look for sympathy in this world! My career has been very interesting; but what's the use of that, if nobody knows it? The world does not deserve to be made acquainted with my history, for it ought to have given me golden shoes, when the emperor's horse was shod, and I stretched out my feet to be shod too. If I had received golden shoes, I should have become an ornament to the stable. Now the stable has lost me, and the world has lost me. It is all over!"

But all was not over yet. A boat, in which there were a few young girls, came rowing up.

"Look, yonder is an old wooden shoe sailing along," said one of the girls.

"There's a little creature bound fast to it," said another.

The boat came quite close to our beetle's ship, and the young girls fished him out of the water. One of them drew a small pair of scissors from her pocket, and cut the woollen thread, without hurting the beetle; and when she stepped on shore, she put him down on the grass.

"Creep, creep—fly, fly—if thou canst," she said. "Liberty is a splendid thing."

And the beetle flew up, and straight through the open window of a great building; there he sank down, tired and exhausted, exactly on the mane of the emperor's favourite horse, who stood in the stable when he was at home, and the beetle also. The beetle clung fast to the mane, and sat there a short time to recover himself.

"Here I'm sitting on the emperor's favourite horse—sitting on him just like the emperor himself!" he cried. "But what was I saying? Yes, now I remember. That's a good thought, and quite correct. The smith asked me why the golden shoes were given to the horse. Now I'm quite clear about the answer. They were given to the horse on my account."

And now the beetle was in a good temper again.

"Travelling expands the mind rarely," said he.

The sun's rays came streaming into the stable, and shone upon him, and made the place lively and bright.

"The world is not so bad, upon the whole," said the beetle; "but one must know how to take things as they come."

Story Analysis

1. Who is the protagonist of the story?

    a) the horse

    b) the beetle

    c) the girls

2. Why did the beetle leave the stable in the beginning of the story?

    a) He wanted to go on an adventure.

    b) He wanted to explore the outside world.

    c) He felt unappreciated at the stable.

3. Where did the beetle find the frogs?

    a) in the flower garden

    b) on the linen

    c) a fragment of pottery

4. Which of these statements about perspective is true according to the excerpt?

> "Is it not beautiful here?" asked one of the little lady-birds that flew about, with their delicate wings and their red-and-black shields on their backs. "How sweet it is here—how beautiful it is!"
>
> "I'm accustomed to better things," said the beetle. "Do you call this beautiful? Why, there is not so much as a dung-heap."

   a) The perception of beauty according to the beetle is a dung-heap, whereas to the lady-birds, it is the flower garden.

   b) The perception of beauty is different for the lady-bird and the beetle, but they see beauty in everything in the world.

   c) The beetle could not agree with the lady-bird as the flower garden was not beautiful.

5. What can we understand about the beetle with this statement?

> Is there never a muck-heap, here in the garden, where a person of rank, like myself, can feel himself at home, and take up his quarters?

   a) The beetle is self-centred and gives itself too much importance.

   b) The beetle is vain and compromises with any situation.

   c) The beetle, though self-admiring, easily adapts to the environment.

6. Which of these encounters in the adventurous journey was the most dangerous for the beetle?

   a) exposure to rain

   b) sail across the ditch

   c) bound to the wooden shoe

7. What point of view is used in this story?

   a) third person objective

   b) third person limited

   c) third person omniscient

8. Where did the beetle settle in the end of the story?

   a) imperial stable

   b) muck-heap

   c) the lake

9. What can be concluded from the beetle's attitude toward the end?

   a) The hardships changed the beetle for the better and made it see goodness in others.

   b) The hardships made the beetle more appreciative and content with what he had.

   c) The hardships that the beetle underwent did not change it for the better.

10. How can we relate the moral of the story to real life?

   a) Learning to explore the world around before we settle for something is a wise decision.

   b) Being jealous of others' achievements and aiming for something higher than that will bring forth success.

   c) Not being appreciative of what we have or being envious of others could be harmful for our well-being.

Character Analysis

Match the characters from the story with their respective character traits.

horse	conceited
beetle	inconsiderate
caterpillar	helpful
gardener's son	appreciative
fly	optimistic
girls	atrocious
ladybugs	loyal

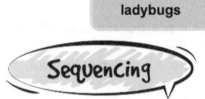

Arrange the following in the order in which they are introduced in the story.

- CATERPILLAR
- EARWIGS
- GIRLS
- FLY
- BEETLE
- FROGS
- BOY
- HORSE

www.prepaze.com

Pirate Story

Three of us afloat in the meadow by the swing,
>Three of us abroad in the basket on the lea.

Winds are in the air, they are blowing in the spring,
>And waves are on the meadow like the waves there are at sea.

Where shall we adventure, today that we're afloat,
>Wary of the weather and steering by a star?

Shall it be to Africa, a-steering of the boat,
>To Providence, or Babylon or off to Malabar?

Hi! but here's a squadron a-rowing on the sea--
>Cattle on the meadow a-charging with a roar!

Quick, and we'll escape them, they're as mad as they can be,
>The wicket is the harbour and the garden is the shore.

---

* by Robert Louis Stevenson

Poem Appreciation

Section A

1. What is the theme of this poem?

   a) love

   b) adventure

   c) courage

2. What is the meadow a metaphor for in this poem?

   > Three of us afloat in the meadow by the swing,

   a) sea

   b) land

   c) air

3. What is the rhyme scheme of the first stanza?

   a) aabc

   b) abab

   c) aabb

4. What is the point of view in this poem?

   a) first person

   b) second person

   c) third person

5. What is the tone of the author in the second stanza?

   a) melancholic

   b) enthusiastic

   c) commiserating

6. What is the figure of speech used in this line?

   > Cattle on the meadow a-charging with a roar!

   a) simile

   b) metaphor

   c) alliteration

Section B

1. Pick out the rhyming words in the second stanza.

Pair 1: _____   _____

Pair 2: _____   _____

2. Pick out a metaphor from the last two lines of the poem.

_____

3. Where are they going to go on adventure in the ship?

_____

Connecting to Text

The children made a ship out of nothing and found happiness in simple things. How do you find happiness in simple things?

_____

Describe any makeshift equipment you made to play with your friends.

_____

What objects around your house can you use to play space station with your friends?

_____

Friend's names and their roles	Objects and how they will be used

Match the Metaphors

Find the metaphors from the poem and match them.

meadow	waves
basket	shore
grass	sea
children	harbor
wicket	ship
garden	pirates

The Moon

Read the poem **The Moon** by Robert Louis Stevenson.

The moon has a face like the clock in the hall;
She shines on thieves on the garden wall,
On streets and fields and harbour quays,
And birdies asleep in the forks of the trees.

The squalling cat and the squeaking mouse,
The howling dog by the door of the house,
The bat that lies in the bed at moon,
All love to be out by the light of the moon.

But all of the things that belong to the day
Cuddle to sleep to be out of her way;
And flowers and children close their eyes
Till up in the morning the sun shall arise.

Read a passage from Wikipedia about the Moon.

The Moon is an astronomical body orbiting Earth as its only natural satellite. The Moon is thought to have formed about 4.51 billion years ago, not long after Earth. The most widely accepted explanation is that the Moon formed from the debris left over after a giant impact between Earth and a hypothetical Mars-sized body called Theia.

The Moon is in synchronous rotation as it orbits Earth; it rotates about its axis in about the time it takes to orbit Earth. This results in it always keeping nearly the same face turned towards Earth. However, because of the effect of liberation, about 59% of the Moon's surface can actually be seen from Earth. The side of the Moon that faces Earth is called the near side, and the opposite the far side. The far side is often inaccurately called the "dark side", but is in fact illuminated as often as the near side: once every 29.5 Earth days. During new moon, the near side is dark.

The slightly greater attraction that the Moon has for the side of Earth closest to the Moon, as compared to the part of the Earth opposite the Moon, results in tidal forces. Tidal forces affect both the Earth's crust and oceans. The most obvious effect of tidal forces is to cause two bulges in the Earth's oceans, one on the side facing the Moon and the other on the side opposite. This results in elevated sea levels called ocean tides. As the Earth spins on its axis, one of the ocean bulges (high tide) is held in place "under" the Moon, while another such tide is opposite. As a result, there are two high tides, and two low tides in about 24 hours.

Comparing Texts

Section A

1. What is the central theme of the poem?

    a) craving of nocturnal creatures

    b) the moon is the most intense celestial body

    c) nightlife and moon

2. What is the main idea of the passage?

    a) formation of the moon from parts of the earth

    b) influence and relationship between the earth and moon

    c) existence of life form on earth due to moon

3. Which choice best describes the author's main purpose in writing the poem?

    a) to entertain

    b) to persuade

    c) to inform

4. Which choice best describes the author's main purposes in writing the passage?

    a) to entertain

    b) to persuade

    c) to inform

5. What is the point of view used in both the texts?

    a) first person

    b) second person

    c) third person

6. Which choice best defines the meaning of the word hypothetical as it is used in the first paragraph of the passage?

    a) fabricated idea or theory

    b) unproved idea or theory

    c) incorrect idea of theory

7. What is the figurative language used in this line?

> The moon has a face like the clock in the hall

   a) alliteration

   b) simile

   c) metaphor

---

8. What is the figurative language used in this line?

> And the flowers and children close their eyes

   a) hyperbole

   b) onomatopoeia

   c) personification

---

9. Which statement would the author of the passage most likely agree with?

   a) The Moon was formed from the debris of Earth and Mars.

   b) A person from earth sees the same face of the moon twice in every 29.5 days.

   c) The moon was formed after the earth was formed.

---

10. Which of the following statements is true according to the poet?

   a) The mouse, bat, and flower belong to the night.

   b) The moon shines on everything that is out in the night.

   c) The cat cannot go out in the daylight, so it is out in the night.

Section B

1. What is the similarity between the passage and poem on the moon?

2. What is the difference between the text and poem on the moon?

3. Which of the two authors required more research?

Word Meaning

Find the meaning of the following words using a dictionary.

satellite

orbit

hypothetical

synchronous

illuminate

tidal

Reading: Informational Text

The Founding Fathers of the USA

The United States of America (USA) is one of the most powerful countries in the world today. If we go back in history, we can see that this country was built by eight great men who are known as the Founding Fathers of the USA. In the late 1800s, many of the top leaders worked together to fight for America's independence from Britain. These leaders also united the 13 separate provinces to build one country – the United States of America.

More than 60 American leaders fought for the independence of America from the rule of Britain's King George III. Of all the leaders, eight of them are considered as the most influential leaders.

1. George Washington

George Washington was the first president of the USA and served the nation from 1789 to 1797. He is known as the "Father of the Nation."

2. Alexander Hamilton

Alexander Hamilton was the first United States Secretary of the Treasury, from 1789 to 1795. He worked to stop the international slave trade.

3. Benjamin Franklin

Benjamin Franklin was not just a politician, but also a scientist and author. He was one of the 5 members who wrote the Declaration of Independence.

4. John Adams

John Adams was a lawyer by profession. He was the second president of the USA and served the country between 1797 and 1801.

5. Samuel Adams

Samuel Adams was John Adam's cousin and a political leader from Massachusetts. He is one of the 56 leaders who signed the Declaration of Independence.

6. Thomas Jefferson

Thomas Jefferson was a lawyer from Virginia who wrote the Declaration of Independence. He was the third president of the USA (1801 to 1809) and the second Vice President of the USA (1797 to 1801.)

7. James Madison

James Madison was also from Virginia. He is known as the "Father of the Constitution" as he played an important role in writing the US constitution. James Madison was the fourth president of the USA, from 1809 to 1817.

8. John Jay

John Jay was a lawyer by profession. He was the first Chief Justice of the USA, from 1789 to 1795. Jay also served as the second governor of New York from 1795 to 1801.

Read and Answer

1. Who are the Founding Fathers of the United States of America?
   _____
   _____

2. Who is known as the Father of the Constitution?
   _____

3. Who is known as the Father of the Nation?
   _____

4. List the first four presidents of the United States of America.
   _____
   _____
   _____

5. Name the two Founding Fathers who came from Virginia.
   _____
   _____

6. Who was the first Chief Justice of the United States of America?
   _____

7. Which of the Founding Fathers was also a scientist?

www.prepaze.com

72

prepaze

Identify the hidden words using the clues given below:

A	V	U	B	D	O	J	T	O	C	W	F
C	B	I	E	J	V	E	M	Y	R	B	J
D	T	C	N	O	A	F	W	A	X	U	N
E	Q	T	I	H	T	F	R	L	A	I	Z
R	S	G	D	N	Z	E	L	J	K	Y	G
A	Q	M	C	J	E	R	E	H	S	V	P
Q	T	P	F	A	Y	S	F	N	O	Z	X
X	L	H	O	Y	G	O	S	G	K	L	A
Q	S	P	K	Z	N	N	D	I	H	B	W
N	O	T	G	N	I	H	S	A	W	I	V
B	J	O	H	N	A	D	A	M	S	X	J
G	R	F	J	Y	F	R	I	L	C	K	W
J	A	M	E	S	M	A	D	I	S	O	N

Clues

1. First president of USA

2. Second president of USA

3. First chief justice of USA

4. Second vice president of USA

5. Fourth president of USA

Fill in the Blanks

Use the correct words from the passage to complete the sentences.

1. _____ was the first United States Secretary of the Treasury.

2. George Washington was the president of the USA from _____ to _____.

3. The leaders united _____ provinces to form one country.

4. Thomas Jefferson was the _____ president of the United States of America.

5. _____ played an important role in writing the constitution of the United States of America.

Word Meaning

Find the meaning of the following words using a dictionary and the context.

Word	Meaning
Constitution	
Treasury	
President	
Province	
Independence	

www.prepaze.com

Pet Survey

Populations from two cities were surveyed about the pets they own. The data collected are reflected in the pie charts below.

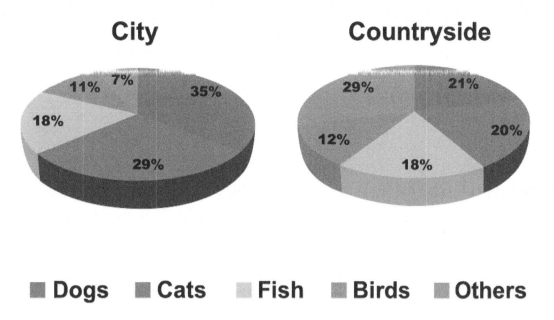

Interpretation of Data

1. In the city, what percentage of the population preferred other animals?

    a) 18%

    b) 12%

    c) 7%

    d) 29%

2. In the countryside, what percentage of the population preferred cats?

    a) 12%

    b) 20%

    c) 21%

    d) 35%

3. Which pet is preferred the least in the countryside?

   a) dogs

   b) cats

   c) fish

   d) birds

4. Which pet is preferred the most in the city?

   a) dogs

   b) cats

   c) fish

   d) birds

5. Which pet is preferred the most in the countryside?

   a) dogs

   b) cats

   c) fish

   d) others

6. Which pet is found at the same amount in the countryside and the city?

   a) dogs

   b) cats

   c) fish

   d) birds

7. How much more dogs are found in the city compared to the countryside?

   a) 14%

   b) 1%

   c) 2%

   d) 18%

8. What is the difference between the percentage of birds found in the countryside and city?

   a) 14%

   b) 1%

   c) 2%

   d) 18%

9. According to the city survey, which of these is arranged in descending order?

a) birds-fish-cats-dogs

b) birds-others-cats-dogs

c) cats-fish-others-birds

d) dogs-cats-birds-others

10. According to the countryside survey, which of these is arranged in ascending order?

a) birds-fish-cats-dogs

b) fish-others-cats-dogs

c) others-dogs-cats-fish

d) dogs-others-birds-fish

Transfer the data from the graph to the below table.

Writing

Narrate an incident where you were kind to someone or someone was kind to you. Follow the 5-step writing process to produce an effective piece of writing.

Complete the organizer with the details pertaining to your narrative.

Who?

When?

Where?

What?

Why?

Step 2: Drafting

Write the essay with the ideas gathered in the planning stage.

Step 3: Editing

Edit the draft above for changes in ideas, grammar, punctuation, and word choice. You can make the changes in a different color pen using the below checklist.

Checklist

- [ ] Does my introduction catch the reader's attention?
- [ ] Does the writing appeal to at least one of the 5 senses?
- [ ] Is there any gap in the narration?
- [ ] Is the verb tense consistent throughout the writing?
- [ ] Are the punctuation marks correctly used in statements and dialogs?
- [ ] Is there repetition of words or ideas?
- [ ] Do I have enough description to provide visual elements?
- [ ] Are the grammar and spelling mistakes checked?
- [ ] Have I capitalized letters that need to be capitalized?
- [ ] Have I used varied sentence structure?

Step 4: Revision

Write the revised draft here with the changes. Feel free to change ideas and sentences.

 Step 5: Publishing/Feedback

Show your work to your parents/siblings and get their feedback. Take both the positive and negative feedback in the same way. Both will help you improve!

Follow this 5-step process for all your writing assignments.

Argumentative Writing

Read the argument between Ian and Casandra. Pick a side and write a 5-paragraph argumentative essay using clear reasons and evidence. You can research to guide you.

I follow a healthy diet. Eating healthy is imperative for human beings.

I don't follow any diet. We live only once! I eat anything that I like.

Explanatory Writing

How often do you read a book and also see a movie adaptation of the same? Isn't it fun to see if the movie adaptation did justice to the book?

Write a 4-paragraph essay comparing a book you read with its movie adaptation.

Complete the organizer for brainstorming:

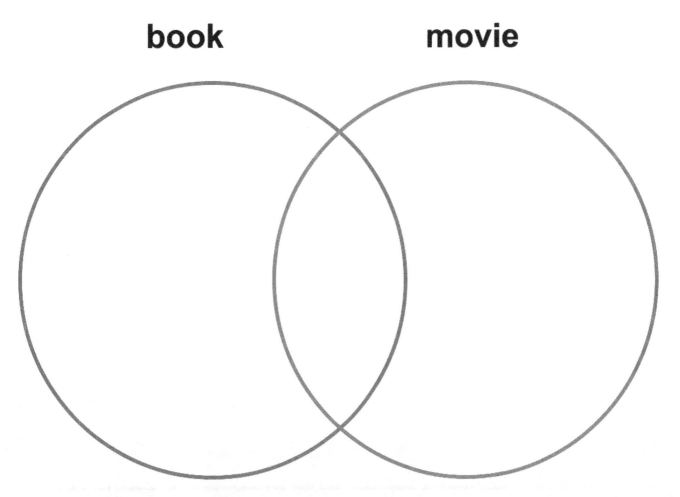

Narrative Writing

Write a story.

➢ Choose a theme and point of view.

➢ Add figurative language.

➢ Follow the structure: a clear beginning, middle, and end.

➢ Give an eccentric title.

Research Writing

Don't you often hear people say, "The President should have done this! The President should have done that"? Do you know what a president of a country is supposed to do?

Write a detailed essay on the roles and responsibilities of a President. Research using print and digital sources.

Remember to follow the 5-step writing process and cite your sources.

Math

Use this book to enable your children to explore numbers by solving interesting puzzles and real-life problems. Engage your children with fun, colorful activities and let them fall in love with Math.

Ratio And Proportional Relationships

A ratio is an ordered pair of non-zero numbers. It is denoted as, $A:B$ to indicate the order of the numbers—the number A is first and the number B is second. The order of the numbers is important to the meaning of the ratio. Switching the numbers changes the relationship.

1. Lessie is a florist. She is making a flower vase. She uses 3 tulips for every 2 roses. Draw her arrangement in the picture below and answer the questions.

a. The ratio of _____ : _____ is 3:2

b. The ratio of _____ : _____ is 3:5

c. The ratio of _____ : _____ is 2:3

Draw here

Fruit Bowl Ratio

2. Look at the fruit bowl and answer the questions.

a) What is the ratio of oranges to strawberries?

b) What is the ratio of strawberries to oranges?

c) What is the ratio of oranges to the total number of fruits?

d) What is the ratio of strawberries to the total number of fruits?

Fun Project At Lego Corp

3. Employees of Lego Corp are doing a fun project with life-size lego blocks. Look at the image and answer the questions.

a. What is the ratio of gray blocks to black blocks?

b. What is the ratio of gray blocks to the total number of blocks?

c. What is the ratio of black blocks to the total number of blocks?

4. Emi's teacher asked her to draw a pattern of triangles and circles to represent the ratio 2 : 3. Emi drew as shown.

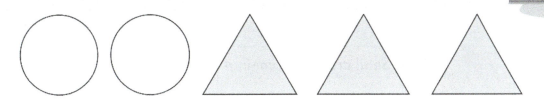

Is Emi correct? Justify.

How Many Stars And Moons?

5. Sean gets stars for every correct answer and moons for every wrong answer. Look at his report of an assessment.

Write the ratio statement to describe his assessment.

How Long Will Miss. Snail Crawl?

6.

Miss. Snail crawls 10 cm in 4 seconds.

a. How far does she crawl in 5 seconds?	b. How long will she take to reach 20 cm?

7. Tom is making apple juice. He needs 12 apples to make 2 bottles of apple juice. Find the unit rate and complete the table.

Number of apples	Bottles of apple juice produced
1	
3	
36	

8. Rhea orders 3 pizzas for 6 people for her birthday party. Answer the questions.

What is the unit rate $\frac{people}{pizza}$?

What is the unit rate $\frac{pizza}{people}$?

If there are 32 people attending the party. How many pizzas should she order?

How many people can she feed with 5 pizzas?

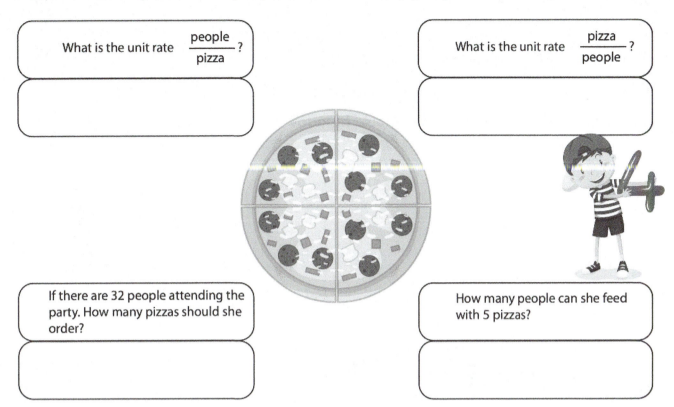

9.

It snows 1/3 of an inch per hour. If 6 inches of snow fell, for how long was it snowing?

10.

The unit rate of blue paint to yellow paint to obtain a shade of green paint is $\frac{1}{5}$. If Kim uses 10 pints of blue paint, how much yellow paint should he add?

How Much Flour?

11. Ronnie is baking cupcakes. Look at the ingredients in her recipe book.

Recipe to make 10 Vanilla Cupcakes

Flour   _   3 cups
Sugar   _   2 cups
Eggs
Baking powder
Baking soda

Answer the questions based on the recipe.

a. To bake 20 cupcakes, how much flour should he use?

b. If he adds 4 cups of sugar, how much flour should he use? How many cupcakes will it yield?

12. Rom makes a fruit punch using oranges and apples.

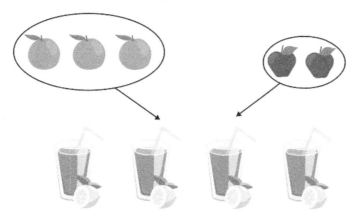

As shown, if he uses 2 apples and 3 oranges to make 4 glasses, complete the table.

	Apple	Orange	Glass of Juices
Original recipe	2	3	4
Double the recipe			
Triple the recipe			
Half the recipe			

13. Look at the given 10 * 10 grid and answer the questions.

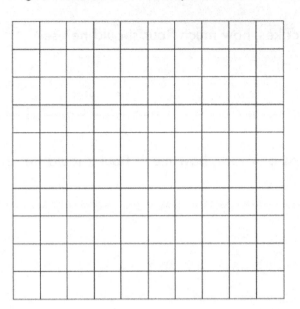

a. If the value of the grid is $50, what is the value of 1 small square in the grid?

b. If the value of the grid is $200, What is the value of 10 small squares in the grid?

c. If the value of a small square is $2, What is the value of the full grid?

d. If the value of 10 squares is $5, What is the value of the full grid?

14. Shade the grids to represent 25% and write the shaded fraction.

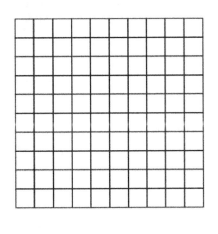
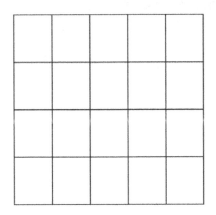
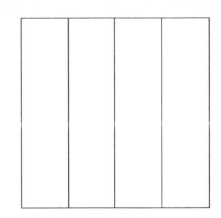

15.

10% of a number is 20.			
a. What is the number?	b. What is 25% of the number?	c. What is 5% of the number?	d. What is 200% of the number?

16. There are 8 ounces in a cup, 2 cups in a pint, and 2 pints in a quart.

a. How many cups are there in 24 ounces?

b. How many ounces are in 2 quarts?

17. Compare the following using >, <, or =.

20 miles per hour		20 km per hour
10 cm per mints		400 m per hours
20 gallons of milk		20 liters of milk
125 kg		125 pounds

18. Write the fraction and percentage for the shaded part of the grids.

Grid	Fraction	Percentage
a		
b		
c		

19. Grade 6 students of Kelly School planned for a farm visit. Lia has created a list of random facts about the visit.

TRIP TO THE FARM

- 60% of the total number of students are girls.
- There are 18 girls in total.
- The distance of the farm from the school is 55 km.
- The bus contractor charges $5 per km.
- The total refreshment for the trip will cost $250.

a. What is the ratio number of boys to girls?

b. What is the cost per head if 2 teachers accompanied the kids?

c. The bus stops 22 km from the school to refill fuel. What percentage of the distance has the bus covered at this point?

Tom's Math Test

20.

a. Tom had correctly answered 22 questions on his math test. He got 88%. How many questions were there in the test?

b. Tom got 24 out of 25 points on his science test. Calculate his percentage.

Number System

1. Kiara has modeled a design for her kitchen countertop.

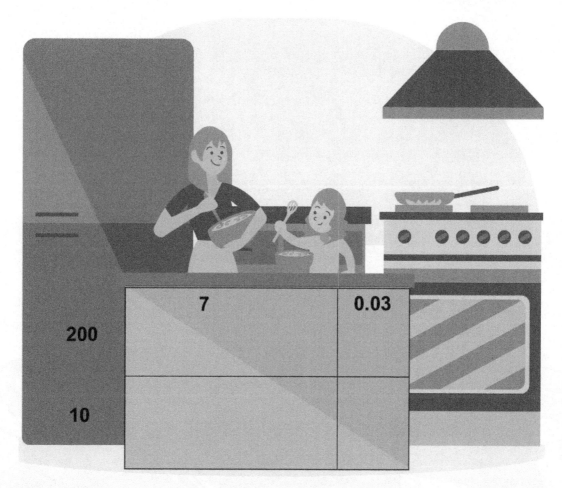

a. What multiplication statement does the numbers represent?

b. Solve the statement.

Help Ryan Floor the Pool

2. A rectangular pool measures 70.25 m X 5 m. Ryan decided to floor it with tiles of side 10 cm X 10 cm. How many tiles does he require to cover the pool?

Traffic Light Mystery

3. The traffic lights at two different road crossings change after every 2 minutes, 3 minutes. If they change simultaneously at 7 a.m., at what time will they change simultaneously again?

4. In a morning walk, three kids step off together. Their steps measure 10 cm, 12 cm, and 9 cm respectively. What is the minimum distance each should walk so that all can cover the same distance in complete steps?

5. Two tankers contain 85 liters and 68 liters of gasoline respectively. Find the maximum capacity of a container which can measure the gasoline of both the tankers when used an exact number of times.

Product Rule for HCF and LCM

6. For the two numbers 24 and 40.

   a. What is the product of the two numbers?

   b. Find their GCD and LCM.

   c. What is the product of their HCF and LCM?

   d. Represent the relationship as a mathematical statement.

Which Is the Best Buy?

7. Juice forest has a summer offer on its juice menu. Which option would you buy for a good deal?

Summer Sale!
Special Price!!

Offer 1

0.48 liters @ $24 only

Offer 2

2.4 liters @ $96.12 only

Offer 3

2.7 liters @ $94.50 only

8. Ria realizes that the number on the house door is divisible by 9, and Ron points out that it is also divisible by 12. What could be the smallest possible number that could be on the house door?

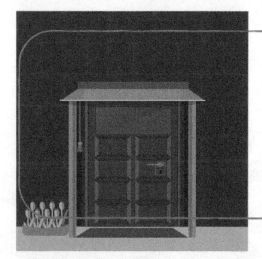

9. Steve buys two types of sandwiches for a school party. One sandwich is 15 inches long and the other sandwich is 18 inches long. Steve has to cut it into individual servings of the same length from both sandwiches without any leftovers. What is the greatest length serving that Steve can cut, and how many pieces will he have now?

10. Identify the given points and state which quadrant they belong to.

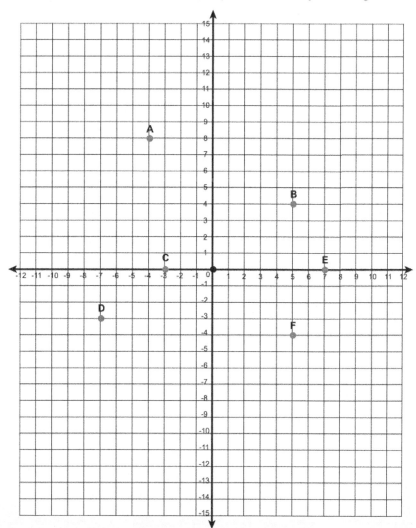

Point	Quadrant
A	
B	
C	
D	
E	
F	

11. Arrange the following rational numbers in order from least to greatest.

1/3, 0.5, 2/5, 3.25, 1 ½, -2.1

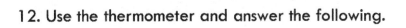
Mark the Temperatures

12. Use the thermometer and answer the following.

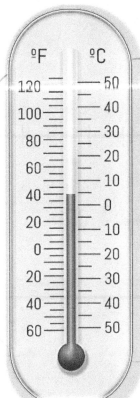

a. Mark the given temperatures on the thermometer, use the corresponding letters.

A = 70°F

B = 12°C

C = 110°F

D = −4°C

b. What is the reading in the given thermometer in °F and °C?

_____

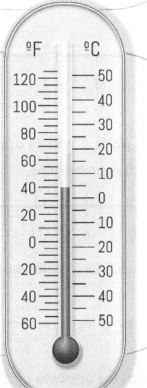

13. Write the integer that represents the opposite for the given values and mark them on the number line.

   a. Gain of $6 _____

   b. Deposit of $10 _____

   c. Loss of $5 _____

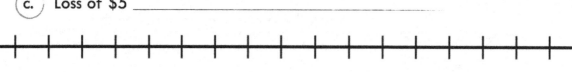

14. Find the distance between the two points on the number line.

a.
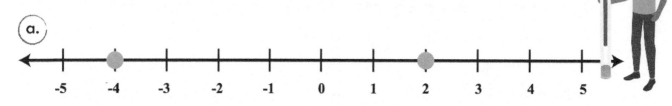

b.
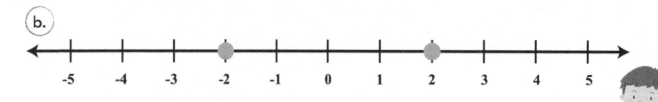

15. Identify the point 5 and its opposite on the number line. Also identify 3 and its opposite on the number line.

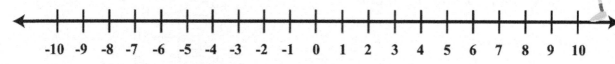

   a. Where does 3 lie in relation to 5 _____

   b. Where does -3 lie in relation to 5 _____

   c. Where does the opposite of 5 lie in relation to 3 _____

Expressions and Equations

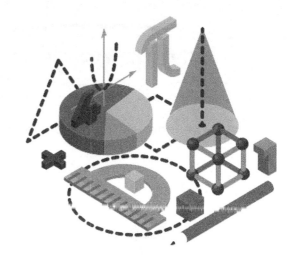

An equation is a statement where the values of two mathematical expressions are equal.

Example:

$6 + 2 = 8$ is an equation. The left side of the equal to sign and the right side of the equal to sign are the same.

Some equations use variables when the quantity is unknown.

Example: $3 + x = 5$

An inequality compares two values, showing if one is less than, greater than, or not equal to another value.

$a \neq b$ means a is not equal to b

$a < b$ means a is less than b

$a > b$ means a is greater than b

$a \leq b$ means that a is less than or equal to b

$a \geq b$ means that a is greater than or equal to b.

Solve the Inequalities

1. Solve the inequalities in the space provided.

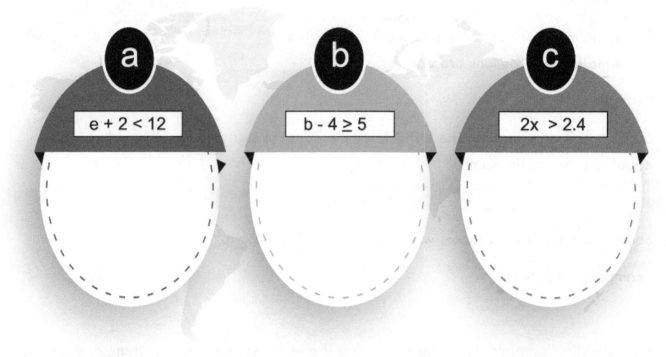

a. $e + 2 < 12$

b. $b - 4 \geq 5$

c. $2x > 2.4$

2. Draw a graph for each inequality.

a. $r \leq -3$

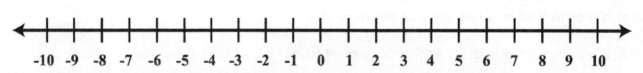

b. $k \geq 6$

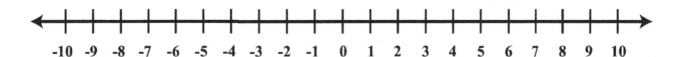

c. $-5 > v$

Determine the Solution

3. Determine whether $x = 8$ is a solution to each of the following inequalities.

a. $2x > 8$

b. $\frac{x}{4} \leq 1$

c. $16 \leq 4x + 4$

d. $x + 1 < 10$

4. Each hanger image represents a balanced equation. Identify the equation.

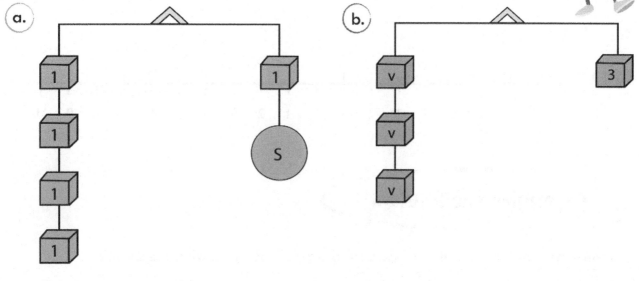

Equation: _____   Equation: _____

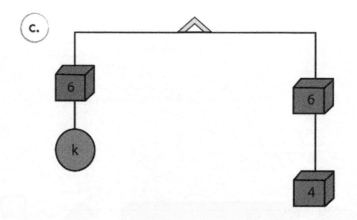

Equation: _____

What Is the Inequality?

5. State the inequality modeled in the number line.

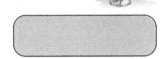

Create Number Sentences

6. Create a number sentence using the given variable and symbol, such that the number sentence should be true for the given value of the variable.

Variable	Symbol	For the value	Number sentence
c	$\geq$	The sentence is true when 5 is substituted for c.	
x	$\neq$	The sentence is true when 10 is substituted for x.	
n	$<$	The sentence is true when 9 is substituted for n.	

True or False?

7. Substitute the value into the variable and state whether the number sentence is true or false.

a. $3\dfrac{5}{6} = 1\dfrac{2}{3} h$, when $h = 2\dfrac{1}{6}$. _____

b. $\dfrac{f}{4} \leq 3$, when $f = 12$. _____

c. $121 - 98 \geq r$, when $r = 23$. _____

d. $\dfrac{54}{q} = 6$, when $q = 10$. _____

Can Richard Play In The Ball Pit?

8. Read the statement and answer the questions.

Richard must be less than 36 inches tall to play in the ball pit at a birthday party.

a. Give some values for the height he can be and enter the ball pit.

b. Write an inequality to represent the height of kids who can play in the ball pit.

c. Give some values for the heights that he cannot play in the ball pit.

d. Stephie is 48 inches tall. Can she play in the ball pit?

e. Create a number line diagram to represent the heights of the children who can play in the ball pit.

9. Start with the given equation. Apply the action to construct an equivalent equation. One is done for you.

Equation	Action	Equivalent equation
X = 6	Add 2 to both sides of the equation.	X + 2 = 8
X = 10	Multiply 5 to both sides of the equation.	
X = 24	Divide both sides of the equation by 4.	
X = 9	Multiply both sides of the equation by 6.	
5 = x	Subtract both sides of the equation by 5.	

10. Solve word problems.

a. The expression to convert Celsius to Fahrenheit, is given. If the temperature is 78 degrees Fahrenheit, what is the temperature in degrees Celsius?

$C = \frac{5}{9}(F-32)$

b. The sixth-grade students are going on a field trip. The field trip costs $6 per student. How many students went on the field trip if the school spent $198 on tickets?

c. Ricky has forty-five baseball cards. If five cards fit on one page of a scrapbook, how many pages does Ricky need to buy for his collection?

d. A group of friends wanted to order T-shirts. The T-shirts cost $20 each plus a shipping fee of $10. The friends did a garage sale to earn money for the shirts. They earned $1,380 at the garage. How many shirts can they order?

11.

a. Make a table of values to evaluate the expression for the value of x given. Then, answer the questions below the table.

Expression: x + 2

i.

x	x + 2
0	
1	
3	
6	

ii. What value for x makes the expression $x + 2$ evaluate to 5?

iii. What value for x makes the expression $x + 2$ evaluate to 7?

b. Make a table of values to evaluate the expression for the value of y given. Then, answer the questions below the table.

Expression: 5y

i.

y	5y
1	
4	
5	
10	

ii. What value for y makes the expression 5y evaluate to 10?

iii. What value for y makes the expression 5y evaluate to 20?

12. Solve each of the equations using the pan balance, a fact family, and isolating the variable. One is done for you.

A number plus two is six.

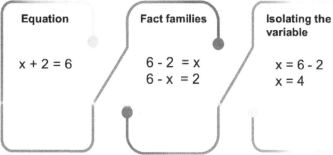

Pan balance:

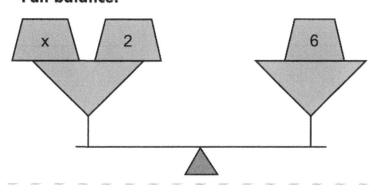

a. Four more than a number is one.

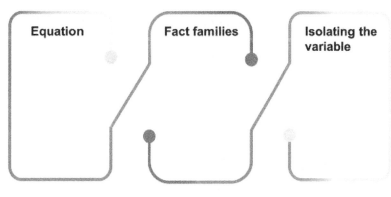

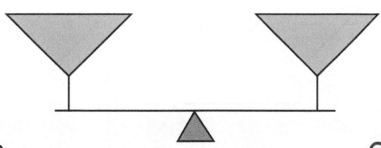

b. Two multiplied by a number is six.

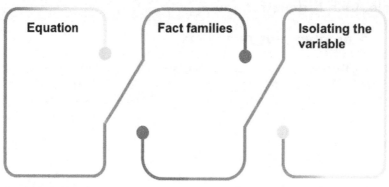

Pan balance:

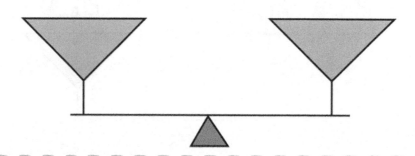

c. Seven times a number is seven.

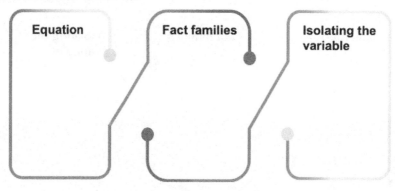

Pan balance:

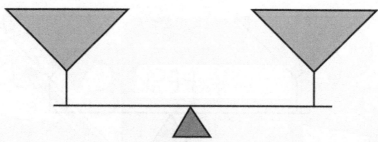

Riddle Time

13. Solve the riddles.

I am thinking of a number, When I divide my number by 5, the result is 8. What number am I thinking of?

I am thinking of a number. When I multiply my number by 4, the result is 24. What number am I thinking of?

Show your working here:

14. Read each story problem. Identify the unknown quantity, and write the addition or subtraction expression that is described. Finally, evaluate your expression using the information given. One is done for you.

Story problem:

David has 5 more dollars than his sister. Write an expression for the amount of money David has.

Description with units:

Let d represent money of David's sister in dollars.

Expression:

Money with David: d + 5

Evaluate the Expression If:

David's sister has $12

Show Your Work and Evaluate:

d + 5

12 + 5 = 17

Thus, David has $17.

a.

Story problem:

Nina read 9 more books than Ben in the first marking period. Write an expression for the number of books Nina read.

Description with units:

Expression:

Evaluate the Expression If:

Ben read 8 books in the first marking period.

Show Your Work and Evaluate:

b.

Story problem:

Felix scored 6 fewer goals than Ivan in the first half of the season. Write an expression for the number of goals Felix scored.

Description with units:

Expression:

Evaluate the Expression If:

Ivan scored 16 goals.

Show Your Work and Evaluate:

Angles at the Parking Lot

15. Emily is designing a parking lot. She has determined that one of the angles should be 115°.

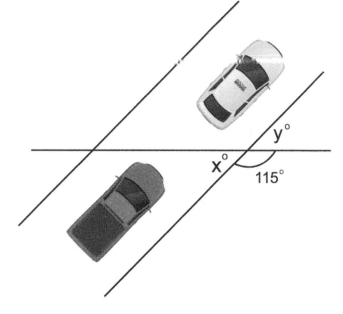

a. What is the measure of angle x and angle y?	
b. How is angle x related to the 115° angle?	
c. How would you solve this equation?	
d. How is angle y related to the angle that measures 115°?	

16. ∠ABC measures 90°. The angle has been separated into two angles.

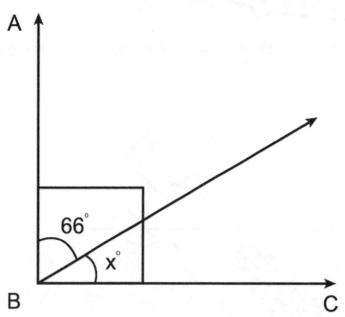

a. If one angle measures 66°, what is the measure of the other angle?

b. How are these two angles related?

c. What equation could we use to solve for x?

17. $\angle ABC$ measures 90°. It has been split into two angles, $\angle ABD$ and $\angle DBC$. The measure of the two angles is in a ratio of 2:1. What are the measures of each angle?

a. Use a tape diagram to represent the ratio 2:1.

b. What is the measure of each angle?

c. How can we represent this situation with an equation?

d. Solve the equation to determine the measure of each angle.

18. Solve for x.

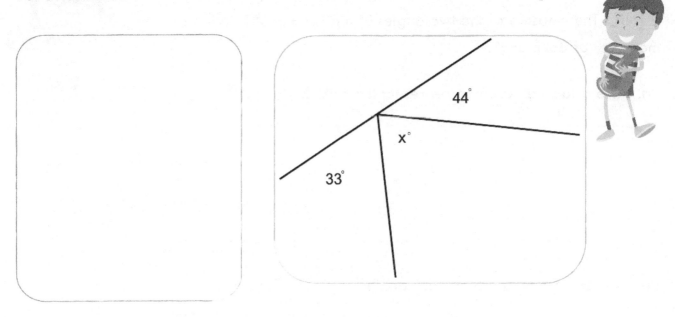

Determine the Tiles to Fit the Corner

19. Elsa is putting in a tile floor. She needs to determine the angles that should be cut in the tiles to fit in the corner. The angle in the corner measures 90°. One piece of the tile will have a measure of 42°. Write an equation, and use it to determine the measure of the unknown angle.

Posters and fliers

20. William designs posters and fliers. He can create three different posters or fliers each week. William wants to create an equation that will give him the total number of posters or fliers he can design given the number of weeks he works.

a. Determine the independent and dependent variables.

b. Create a table to show the number of posters and fliers he can design over the first 5 weeks.

Number of Weeks	Number of poster or fliers designed

c. Write an equation to represent the number of posters and fliers he can design when given any number of weeks.

21. A photographer charges a flat fee of $8 for a 3-hour event plus an additional $2.25 per additional hour.

a. Show the relationship between the total cost and the number of hours.

b. Which variable is independent, and which is dependent?

c. Write an equation to model the relationship, and make a table to show the cost of events with duration from 4 to 10 hours.

Noah's Saving Plan

22. Each week Noah earns $20.

a. If he saves this money, create a graph that shows the total amount of money Noah would save from week 1 through week 10.

Week	Amount saved

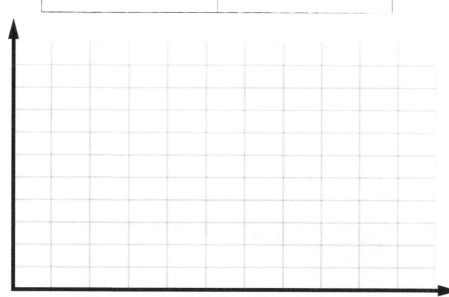

b. Write an equation that represents the relationship between the number of weeks that Noah has saved his money, *w*, and the total amount of money in dollars he has saved, *s*. Then, name the independent and dependent variables.

23. What value(s) does the variable have to represent for the equation or inequality to result in a true number sentence?

a. $d + 7 = 21$ $d =$

b. $e + 8 \geq 31$ $e =$

c. $2f = 30$ $f =$

24. Write an inequality to represent each situation. Then, graph the solution in a number line.

a. Blayton is at most 2 meters above sea level.

b. Logan must-read for a minimum of 30 minutes.

c. Racheal has been working part-time. She earns $20 per hour and needs at least $100 to go to the concert. How many hours should she work now?

Complete the Table

25. Complete the table.

Exponent Form	Series of Product	Standard Form
2^3		
	3 X 3 X 3 X 3	
		1.21
$\left(\dfrac{1}{2}\right)^6$		

26. Use a model to prove that 3(2x + 3y) = 6x + 9y.

Area and Perimeter

27. Create an expression to represent the area and perimeter of the given model.

```
        x         2x          x
      ┌─────┬───────────┬─────┐
   x  │     │           │     │  x
      └─────┴───────────┴─────┘
        x         2x          x
```

28. Evaluate the expression

a. $4^x - 3^y$ for $x = 2$ and $y = 3$

b. $2x(3y-z)$ when $x = \dfrac{1}{2}$ $y = 1$ and $z = -1$

29. The length, breadth, and height of a cuboid are in the ratio 1 : 2 : 3.

a. Create an expression to calculate the volume of the box.

b. What is the volume when its:

length is 4 cm	
breadth is 4 cm	

 Is Ron Right?

30. Ron has simplified the expression: 25 − (4 × 3 + 5).

Step 1 : 25 − (32)

Step 2 : 25 − 32

Step 3 = -7

Is he right?

Geometry

An altitude of a triangle is a perpendicular segment from a vertex of a triangle to the line containing the opposite side. The opposite side is called the base. The height of a triangle is the length of the altitude. The length of the base is called either the base length or, more commonly, the base.

A net is a two-dimensional figure that can be folded into a three-dimensional object.

The formula to calculate the area of a parallelogram is $A = b \times h$, where b represents the base and h represents the height of the parallelogram. The height of a parallelogram is the line segment perpendicular to the base. The height is usually drawn from a vertex that is opposite the base.

The formula to calculate the area of a right triangle is $A = \frac{1}{2} \times b \times h$, where b represents the base and h represents the height of the triangle.

1. Calculate the area of the parallelogram. Note the figure is not drawn to scale.

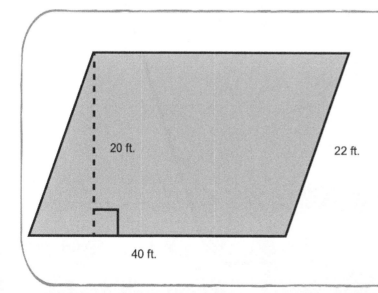

2. Calculate the area of the parallelogram. Note the figure is not drawn to scale.

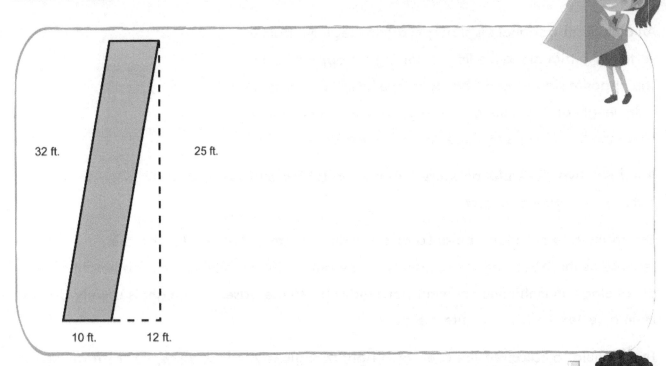

3. Draw and label the height and base of the parallelogram.

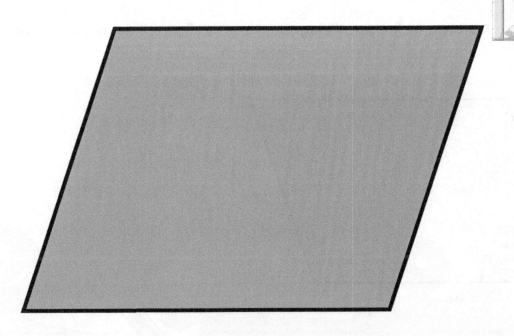

4. Draw and label the height and base of the parallelogram.

5. Do the rectangle and parallelogram below have the same area? Explain why or why not.

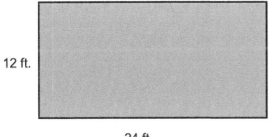

24 ft.

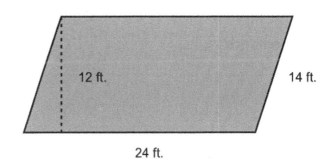

24 ft.

Drek's Swimming Pool

6. Drek is building a triangular swimming pool, as shown below.

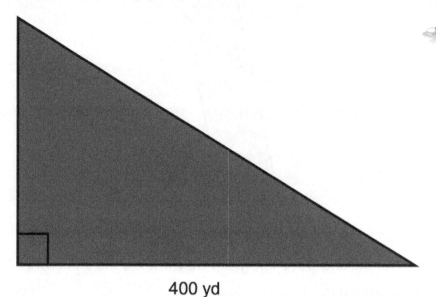

75 yd

400 yd

a. He tiles the base of the pool using tiles of length 1 square yard. How many tiles will he need?

b. He then builds a small garden adjacent to the pool. What will be the area of the garden and pool together?

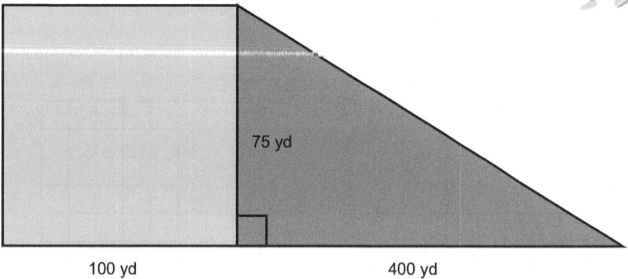

100 yd   400 yd

Lucy's Kitchen Counter

7. Lucy is designing a kitchen counter for her new home. Below is a sketch of two counter she likes when looking at them from above. All measurements are in feet.

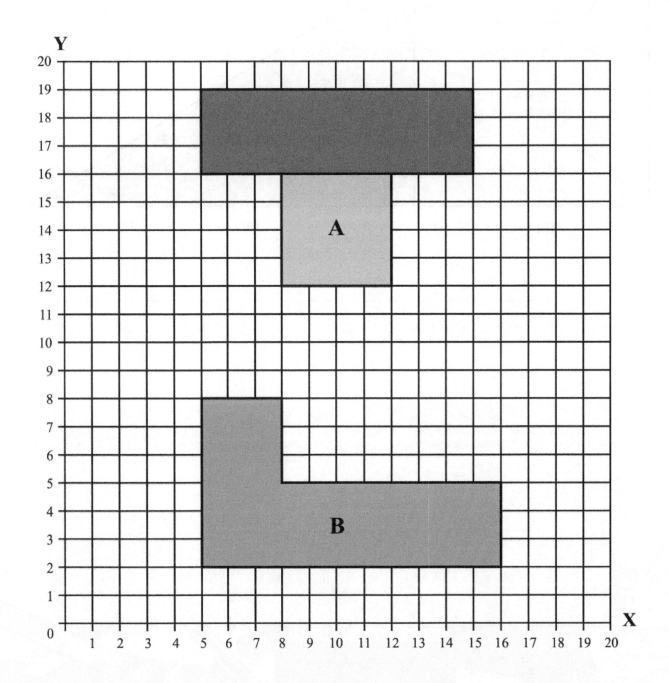

a. If Lucy needs to choose the one with the greater area, which one should she choose? Justify your answer with evidence, using coordinates to determine side lengths.

Counter A	Counter B

b. If Lucy needs to choose the one with the greater perimeter, which one should she choose? Justify your answer with evidence, using coordinates to determine side lengths.

Counter A	Counter B

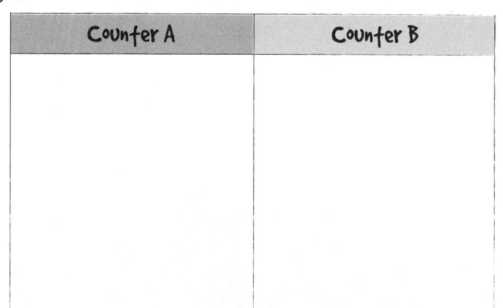

8. Find the area of the triangular region.

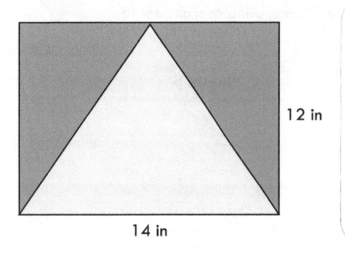

Area of a School

9. The grid below shows a bird's-eye view of a middle school.

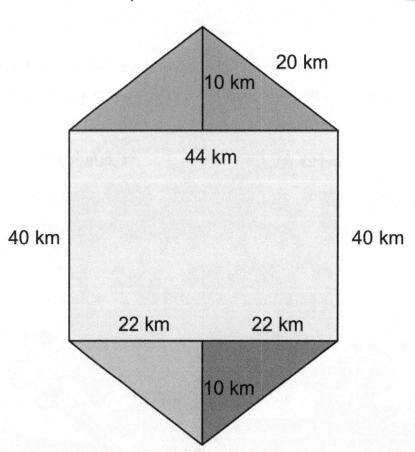

a. Calculate the area of each part of the school.

b. Calculate the area of the whole school.

10. Answer the questions using this rectangular prism.

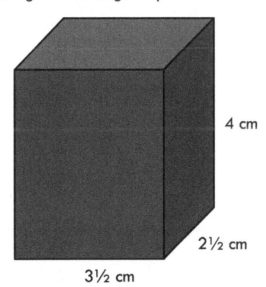

4 cm
2½ cm
3½ cm

a. What is the volume of the prism?

b. Faye fills the rectangular prism with cubes of side lengths of $\frac{1}{2}$ cm. How many cubes does she need to fill?

c. How is the number of cubes related to the volume?

d. Why is the number of cubes needed different than the volume?

11. A fruit vendor is packing the fruits inside the cube-shaped box with side lengths of $6\frac{1}{2}$ in. This box is then gift-wrapped into a box with dimensions 16 in. x 13 in. x $6\frac{1}{2}$ in.

a. Determine the volume of both the boxes.

b. How many fruit boxes can be packed in the gift box?

An Aquarium Math Problem

12. A rectangular aquarium has a volume of 64.224 cubic meters. The height is 4.2 meters and the length is 6.4 meters.

a. Write an equation that relates the volume to the length, height, and width. Let w represent the width in meters.

b. Find the width.

13. Plot the points and determine the area of the polygon.

A(-3, 5) B(2,5) C(-1, -2) D(-6,-2)

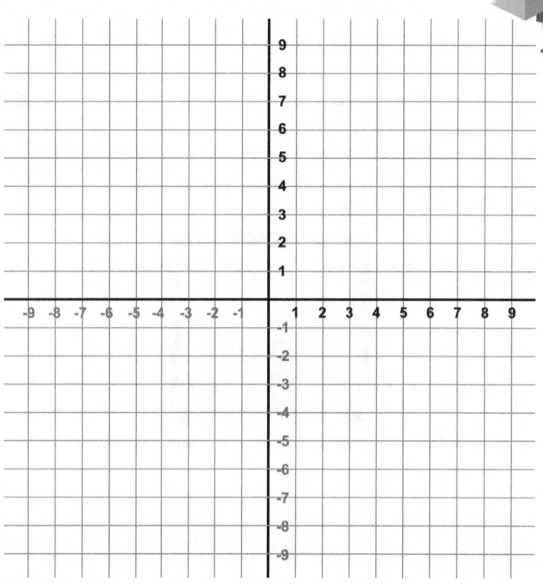

14. A rectangle with two vertices located at (5, -8) and (5,4) has an area of 72 square units. Determine the location of the other two vertices.

Football Ground Math Problem

15. The grid below shows the birds-eye view of a football ground.

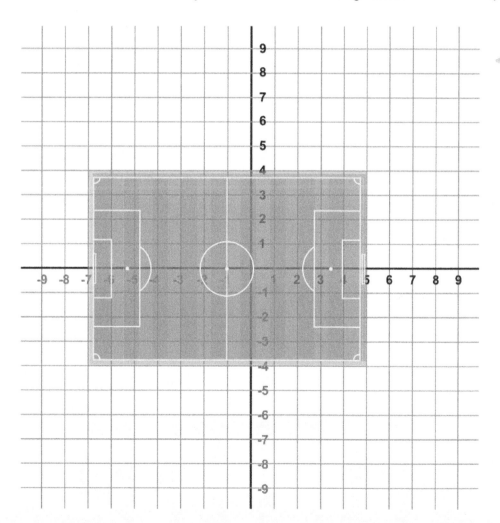

a. Mark and write the coordinates of each point of the football ground in the table.

Points	Coordinates

b. Each space on the grid stands for 10 meters. Find the length of each side of the ground.

c. Find the area of the entire ground.

Fun Math Activity

▷ Trace the figure given in a sheet of paper.

▷ Fold along the dotted lines.

▷ Cut at the highlighted part.

▷ Overlap the folded parts.

▷ Insert the ears of the rabbit at the cut.

▷ A cute box is ready for use.

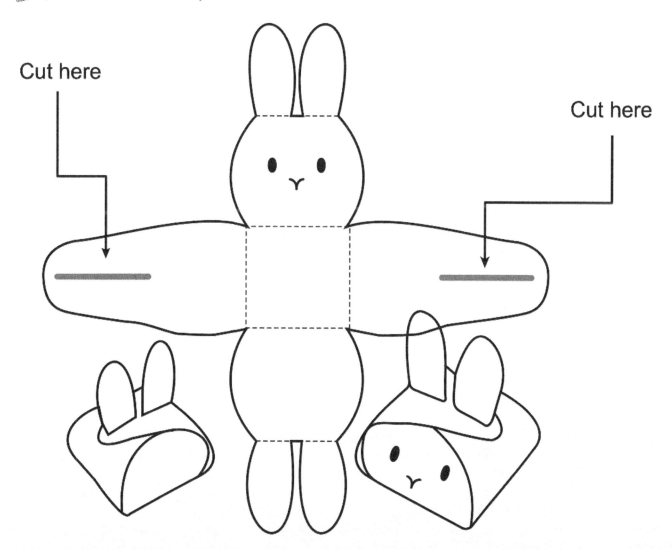

Cut here

Cut here

A Juicy Problem

16. Sketch and label the net of the following solid figures, and label the edge lengths.

a. An orange juice pack that measures 12 inches high, 6 inches long, and 3 inches wide.

b. A banana juice pack 7 inches on each side with a base 5 inches and width 3 inches.

17. Name the shape, and write an expression for surface area. Calculate the surface area of the figure. Assume each box on the grid paper represents a 1 ft. × 1 ft. square.

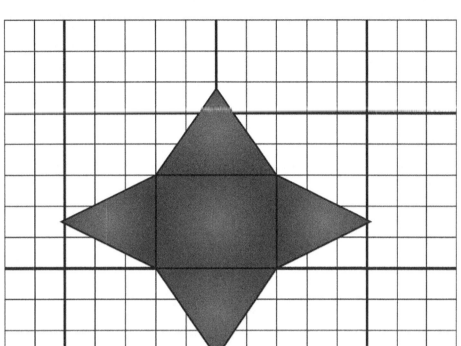

Surface area:

Help Jessica Make Gift Boxes

18. Jessica is making gift boxes for her sister's birthday. She wants how many different-sized boxes having a volume of 20 cubic centimeters she can make if the dimensions must be whole centimeters.

a. List all the possible whole number dimensions for the box.

b. Which possibility requires the least amount of material to make?

c. Which box would you recommend her to use? Why?

Statistics and Probability

Statistics is about using data to answer questions. A statistical question is one that can be answered by collecting data and where there will be variability in the data. Two types of data are used to answer statistical questions: numerical and categorical.

A relative frequency is the frequency for an interval divided by the total number of data values. A relative frequency histogram is a histogram that is constructed using relative frequencies instead of frequencies.

A data distribution can be described in terms of its center, spread, and shape. The center can be measured by the mean. The spread can be measured by the mean absolute deviation (MAD). A dot plot shows the shape of the distribution

Categorical or Numerical Data Sets

1. Identify each of the following data sets as categorical (C) or numerical (N). Explain your answer.

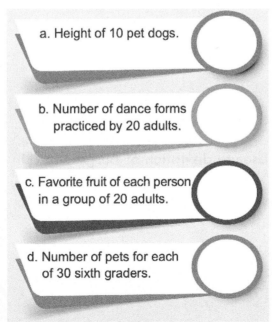

a. Height of 10 pet dogs.

b. Number of dance forms practiced by 20 adults.

c. Favorite fruit of each person in a group of 20 adults.

d. Number of pets for each of 30 sixth graders.

www.prepaze.com

Lunch Hour at Big Burgers

2. The following table lists, the number of burgers sold at Big Burgers in a week during lunch hours.

Day of the week	Number of burgers sold
Monday	350
Tuesday	300
Wednesday	325
Thursday	340
Friday	400
Saturday	250
Sunday	450

a. Calculate the mean number of burgers sold in a week.

b. Calculate the mean absolute deviation of burgers sold in a week.

The following table displays data on calories for different types of burgers.

Burger type	Calories
Cheeseburger	295
Double cheeseburger	417
Triple cheeseburger	796
Chilli burger	409
Soy burger	125
Veggie burger	124
Turkey burger	160
Ground beef burger	230

c. Round the calories values to the nearest 100 calories, and use these rounded values to produce a dot plot of the distribution of the calories.

d. Describe the distribution of the calories.

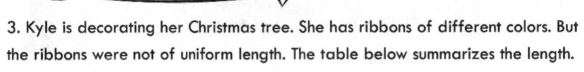 

Kyle's Christmas Tree

3. Kyle is decorating her Christmas tree. She has ribbons of different colors. But the ribbons were not of uniform length. The table below summarizes the length.

Length (in meter)	Frequency
10.00 - <10.25	5
10.25 - <10.50	6
10.50 - <10.75	7
10.75 - <11.00	3
11.00 - <11.25	2
11.25 - <11.50	7
11:50 - <11.75	6
11.75 - <12.00	1
12.00 - <12.25	5
12.25 - <12.50	4

a. Create a histogram for these data.

b. Describe the shape of the histogram you created.

c. Without calculating the mean length, explain based on the histogram whether the mean board length should be equal to 11 meters, greater than 11 meters, or less than 11 meters. Explain what strategy you used to determine this.

d. Based on the histogram, should the mean absolute deviation (MAD) be larger than 0.25 meters or smaller than 0.25 meters? Explain how you made this decision.

A Science Experiment

4. Mark is recording how long it takes water to freeze into ice at a particular temperature. He makes 5 trials. The mean time for the five trials is 3.75 minutes.

a. What is the total time for the five trials?

b. Mark notices the timer malfunctioned on one of the five trials. The result of the trial had been recorded to be 4.6 seconds. If you remove that time from the list and recompute the mean for the remaining four times, what do you get for the mean? Show your work.

What's your favorite flavor?

5. A group of adults were asked how many flavors of ice cream they have had in the past year. Below is the dot plot of their response.

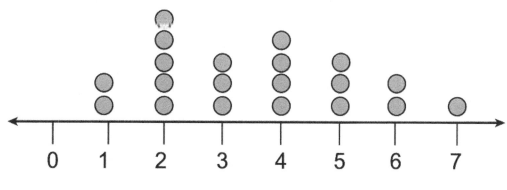

Number of flavors

a. How many observations are in this data set?

b. In a few sentences, summarize this distribution in terms of shape, center, and variability.

c. Based on the dot plot above and without doing any calculations, circle the best response below, and then explain your reasoning.

A. I expect the mean to be larger than the median.

B. I expect the median to be larger than the mean.

C. The mean and median should be similar.

Explain:

d. To summarize the variability of this distribution, would you recommend reporting the interquartile range or the mean absolute deviation? Explain your choice.

e. Suppose everyone in the original data set has had one new flavor in the past one year. Without doing any calculations, describe how the following values would change (i.e., larger by, smaller by, no change—be specific).

Mean:
Median:
Mean Absolute Deviation:
Interquartile Range:

6. If a class of 31 students had a mean of 80 on a test, interpret the mean of 80 in the sense of a fair share measure of the center of the test scores.

7. Dot plots for the amount of time it took workers of Koolz industries and Karz mechanics to reach their workplace are given.

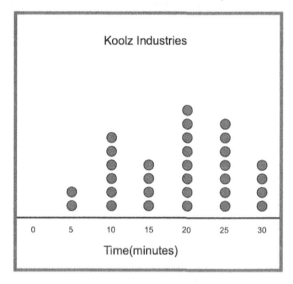

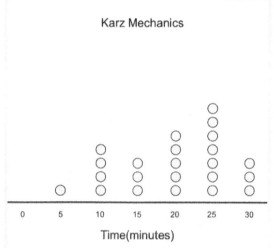

a. Make a box plot for each company.

Koolz Industries

Karz Mechanics

b. What is one thing you can see in the dot plot that you cannot see in the box plot? What is something that is easier to see in the box plot than in the dot plot?

How Many Pets Does Noah's Friends Have?

8. Noah asked his friends how many pets each had. Their responses were 3, 4, 3, 2, 1. Noah showed the data with cubes as follows:

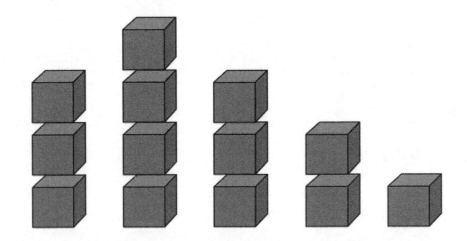

a. Represent the data in a data plot.

b. Noah does a fair share step by having his friend with four pets share one of his pets with one of the children with two pets.

c. Draw the cubes representation that shows the result of this fair share step.

d. Draw the dot plot that shows the result of this fair share step.

9. The following table lists the total area (in sq. km) of ten countries.

Country	Total Area (sq. km)
Russia	1,70,98,242
Canada	99,84,670
China	97,06,961
United States	93,72,610
Brazil	85,15,767
Australia	76,92,024
India	32,87,590
Argentina	27,80,400
Kazakhstan	27,24,900
Algeria	23,81,741

a. Calculate the five-number summary (minimum, lower quartile, median, upper quartile, and maximum) of the total areas. Be sure to include measurement units with each value.

b. Calculate the interquartile range (IQR) for the total area.

c. Draw a box plot of the total area.

d. Would you classify the distribution as roughly symmetric or skewed? Explain.

10. The dot plot shows the number of popcorn kernels in a sample of twenty large bags from a cineplex.

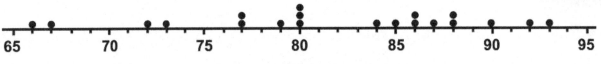

Number of popcorn kernels

Which of the following statement(s) would seem to be true for the given data? Explain your reasoning.

a. Half of the bags had more than 82 kernels in them.

b. Half of the bags had fewer than 82 kernels in them.

c. More than half of the bags had more than 82 kernels in them.

d. More than half of the bags had fewer than 82 kernels in them.

e. If you got a random bag of kernels, you could get as many as 93 kernels.

Science

Help your children learn and enjoy a wide range of information and fun facts that will surprise and amaze them. Find numerous Science experiments, cool facts, activities, and quizzes for the children to enjoy learning.

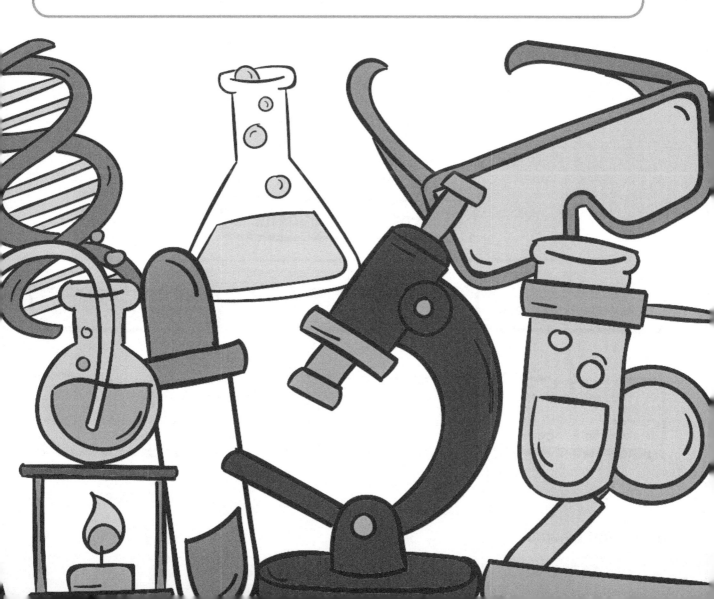

Earth Sciences - Plate Tectonics and Earth's Structure

Tectonic Plates

Earth's interior is made of many layers, starting from the crust, upper mantle which makes the lithosphere, aesthenosphere, lower mantle and the core. The lithosphere is broken into several large pieces which form the lithospheric plates. These lithospheric plates are in constant motion. At the boundaries of these plates, there are different types of motions that can occur. Based on these movements, the boundaries are classified into three types:

- Convergent boundary
- Divergent boundary
- Transform fault boundary

Lithospheric Plates

Convergent boundary	Divergent boundary	Transform fault boundary
A lithospheric plate boundary where two plates come together	A lithospheric plate boundary where two plates move away	A lithospheric plate boundary where two plates slide past each other

The movement in these boundaries leads to mountain formation, deep ocean trenches, valleys, earthquakes, tsunamis, and volcanoes.

Earthquakes in particular, are caused when there is movement of plates along the transform fault boundaries. The movement of the lithospheric plates causes buildup friction between the two plates which causes the earthquake. There are different parts of an earthquake that one must know to analyze. Useful information can be deduced for better understanding.

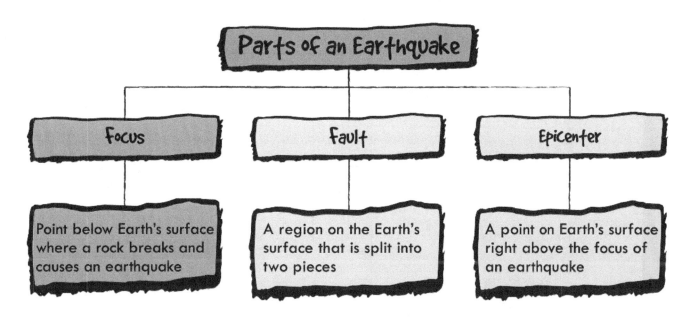

Earthquakes are detected by detecting seismic waves that are generated. There are two types of waves - Body waves that travel through the interior of Earth and Surface waves which are body waves reaching the surface traveling along Earth's surface.

Crossword

Complete the crossword using the clues given below.

Across	Down
2. long chains of undersea mountains	1. lithospheric plates move over this region
3. an ancient supercontinent	3. a theory explaining how the pieces of Earth's surface move
4. a valley formed on ocean floor due to collision of oceanic plates	5. the process of lithospheric plate sinking into the mantle
7. an idea that the continents move around on Earth's surface	6. a lithospheric plate that forms the floor of the ocean

Causes and Effects of Plate Boundaries

Complete the table with details about plate boundaries.

Name of the plate boundaries	What causes it?	What are the effects?

Name of the plate boundaries	What causes it?	What are the effects?
Name of the plate boundaries	What causes it?	What are the effects?

Tectonic Plates Around the World

Identify and label the following major tectonic plates in the map given below.

1. Pacific plate
2. Indo-Australian plate
3. Antarctic plate
4. Eurasian plate
5. African plate
6. American plate

www.prepaze.com

prepaze

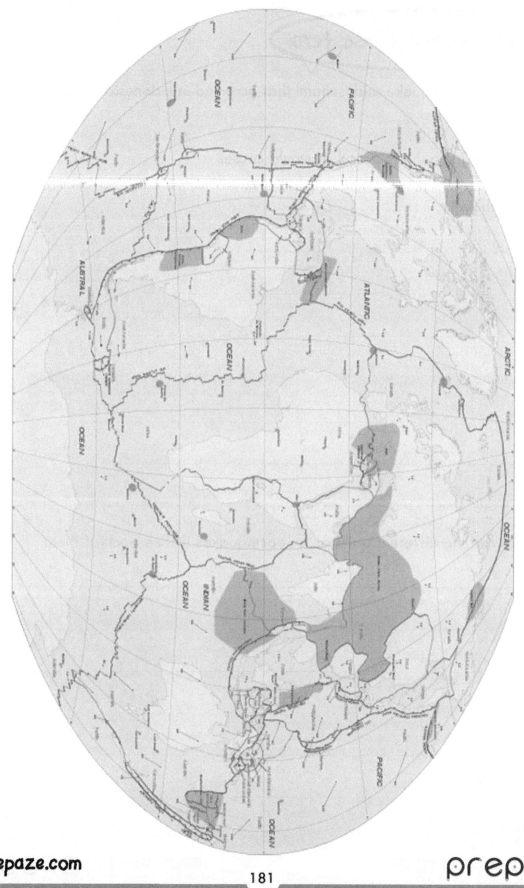

Research on Natural Disasters

Research on the earthquake and tsunami that occurred in Indonesia in the year 2018.

1. List and explain the factors that would cause:

    a. an earthquake

    _____
    _____
    _____

    b. a tsunami

    _____
    _____
    _____

2. What are the different parts of an earthquake? Define each of them.

    _____
    _____
    _____
    _____
    _____
    _____

3. List the following about the Indonesian earthquake and tsunami in September 2018.

   a. Name of the fault line:

   b. What was the height of the tsunami wave caused by the earthquake?

   _____

   c. What was the magnitude of the earthquake?

   _____

   d. Print out a map of Indonesia and locate the epicenter of the earthquake. Paste the map in the space provided.

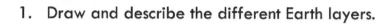
Layers of the Earth

1. Draw and describe the different Earth layers.

2. Rachel has written a story on the journey to the center of the Earth. Here are some statements from her story. Identify if each of the statements are TRUE or FALSE. Correct the false statements and rewrite them in the space provided below.

A. It gets hotter toward the center of the Earth. _____

B. The temperature of the inner core is about 100°C. _____

C. The center of the Earth is solid. _____

D. The distance to the center of the Earth is about 400 km. _____

E. The aesthenosphere is a part of the upper mantle. _____

_____

_____

_____

_____

Faults and Earthquakes

Answer the following questions.

1. Write the clues to finding transform faults.

   _____
   _____
   _____
   _____
   _____
   _____

2. Which is a well-known fault in the United States of America that is known to cause a lot of earthquakes? Mention the lithospheric plates where you can find the fault.

   _____
   _____
   _____
   _____

Analyze an Earthquake

Answer the following questions.

1. Differentiate body waves from surface waves.

Body Waves	Surface Waves

2. Which wave is recorded first by the seismograph and which is the second wave? Why?

_____

_____

_____

_____

_____

3. Given here is a sample data for finding an earthquake epicenter.

Station Name	S-P wave time difference (in seconds) – x axis	Distance to epicenter (in km) – y axis
A	30	110
B	35	130
C	40	150

a. Plot the points given in the table on the graph given below. Use the seismic time-distance graph below to convert the time differences into distances to the epicenter.

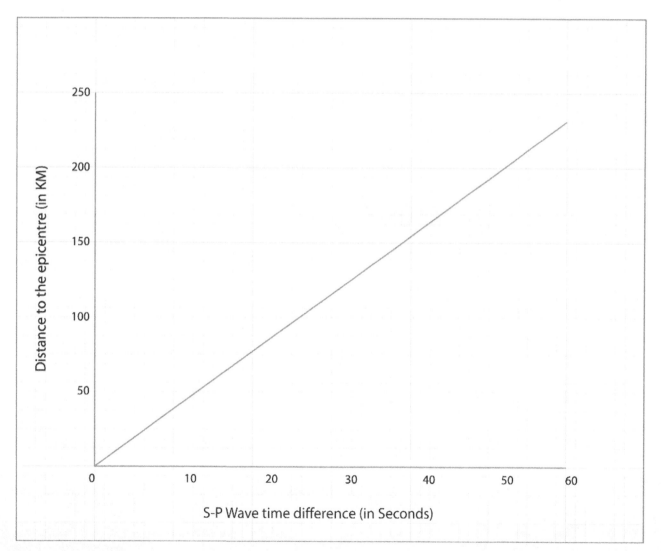

b. Draw a circle around the location of each seismic station and find the epicenter of the earthquake. Mark the epicenter.

(Hint: Deduce the radius of the circles to be drawn from the map you just plotted above.)

Earth Sciences - Shaping Earth's Surface

Factors That Shape the Earth

Wind, air, and water together cause weathering of rocks outside the Earth's surface. The process of breaking down rocks by natural elements is called weathering. Weathering can be two main types.

Physical Weathering - caused by wind and water. Some of the ways rocks can be weathered by water are frost wedging and glaciers. Wind moves broken and chipped rock bits and erodes them.

Chemical Weathering - caused by gases in the air mixed with water which erode rock surfaces.

Rocks can be subject to both types of weathering at the same time.

Some of the other ways rocks are broken down are root wedging and rockfalls.

Rivers flow down mountains cutting valleys, flow on the plains as meanders depositing sediments collected on their way, join the oceans depositing more sediments which form the delta.

Shaping the Surface of the Earth

Find the words in the word grid given to fill in the blanks.

1. The process of breaking rock is called _____.

2. _____ is a process where frozen water inside cracks present in rocks cause it to break down.

3. Frozen water which grinds the valley floor with pieces of rocks lodged in it are called _____.

4. Old statue surfaces have been worn away due reactions between water and the rock surface in the process of _____.

5. Plants growing roots into small crevices and exert force on the rock. This breaks down the rocks into smaller pieces. This process is called _____.

6. Small pieces and grains of weathered rocks formed by flowing rivers are called _____.

7. Grains settling in order, based on their size due to the flow of water is called _____.

8. A stream that has many channels that criss-cross each other is called a _____.

9. S-shaped curves formed by rivers are called _____.

H	H	N	F	M	R	G	R	E	D	E	D	S	A	W	E	N	I	N	G
B	R	I	R	N	G	W	T	E	R	I	S	A	U	Y	U	P	G	P	O
B	N	M	O	J	X	L	N	E	F	G	H	J	Z	C	O	N	S	S	D
H	I	L	S	K	T	V	Y	N	H	G	R	D	B	M	I	N	E	J	X
W	E	A	T	H	E	R	I	N	G	V	E	T	N	R	E	Y	D	K	A
A	I	M	W	E	D	A	T	N	O	O	N	E	E	M	E	A	I	L	O
U	B	N	E	B	D	J	E	K	F	G	K	H	S	A	L	D	M	S	P
D	B	N	D	W	Q	O	P	M	L	N	T	J	V	E	Y	N	E	R	L
B	R	I	G	D	N	J	I	K	M	A	L	S	N	R	S	N	N	E	L
H	K	N	I	B	B	T	R	I	E	H	A	L	P	T	A	I	T	I	X
O	V	M	N	I	A	Q	L	W	H	K	U	N	V	S	I	K	S	C	D
B	L	B	G	J	I	D	L	C	R	O	S	S	C	D	U	R	T	A	L
R	A	M	N	A	G	A	R	V	A	D	A	V	A	E	E	L	L	L	I
D	E	M	O	N	C	T	Y	R	O	O	T	W	E	D	G	I	N	G	K
N	A	L	V	I	A	R	N	A	G	A	R	I	N	I	L	O	O	K	I
M	E	R	M	S	A	L	K	I	T	H	A	A	B	A	B	A	I	L	I
N	A	E	G	N	I	D	D	E	B	D	E	D	A	R	G	S	A	R	K
G	H	U	M	M	U	N	U	P	O	M	D	A	V	B	E	N	N	A	I
C	O	C	A	R	O	K	O	N	U	K	O	H	B	I	T	Y	L	A	Q

Journey through the Meander

Imagine you are a water droplet. Draw and describe your journey in a meander. Add details of experience as a fast moving water droplet and a slow moving water droplet.

Types of Rocks

State whether the following statements are true or false. If false, rewrite them correctly.

1. Clay and silt are the finest particles which together form sandstone.

2. Mudstone is formed from pebbles and silt.

3. Limestone is formed from years of hardened dead marine plants and animals.

4. The order in which sedimentary rock layers are formed from larger to smaller is called cross bedding.

5. In a graded bedding pattern, the finest particles are at the bottom.

6. When sediment settles on the bottom of the lake, the larger pieces settle last.

7. Young mountains have rounded tops with vegetation while old mountains have sharp peaks with no vegetation.

8. Water is both a physical and chemical weathering agent.

9. Longshore drift occurs when waves move toward and away from a beach along the same path.

10. Submarine canyons prevent loss of sand at beaches.

Complete the crossword.

Across	Down
3. Flat land near a river that tends to flood	1. When water overwhelms a normal dry land
5. Ground sliding as soil particles get surrounded by water	2. Unwanted fire that burns in a forest
7. These volcanoes release runny lava	3. Quick heavy rainfall where the land cannot absorb water
9. Fine particles of cooled magma	4. Measures seismic waves
11. Natural hazard driven by Earth's internal energy	6. Occurs when soil conducts seismic waves
	8. Caused by sudden movements of sea floor
	10. Wind that blows over 74 miles per hour

Journey in a Lahar

Draw and describe your journey in a Lahar. Include the start and end points of your journey in your description.

Create a Report

Research a recent hurricane and complete the report given below.

Key facts about the hurricane

Name of hurricane	
Date hurricane occurred	
Location(s)	
Maximum wind speed	
Hurricane category	

Impacts of the Hurricane

Death toll	
Structural damage caused	
Homeless count	

Environmental impacts (mention about animal habitats affected on land and coasts)	

What was done to help?

a. What was done before the hurricane occurred?

Hint - Mention details about alerts, precautions taken to save people and property

_____

_____

_____

_____

_____

b. What help was given to people who lost homes and businesses?

_____

_____

_____

_____

Earth Sciences – Energy in the Earth System

Sun – Major Source of Energy for Weather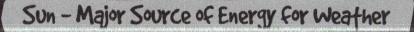

Wind, water, and temperature together create Earth's weather patterns. Weather is the condition of the atmosphere in terms of temperature, atmospheric pressure, and wind. Sun's heat energy warms up the Earth's surface. The heated air becomes less dense and rises, while the cooler air sinks down to get heated up and rise. This happens as a cycle and creates thermals. Thermals are small convection currents that occur in the atmosphere.

The Sun's heat energy not only heats up landforms, but also water (in all forms). The warm air crosses oceans to flow over mountain tops. Cooler temperatures on mountain tops cool down the warm air with water vapor in it, thereby leading cloud formation. This further cools down and pours down as rain. The rain fills up lakes, ponds, and other water bodies on Earth. Sun's heat evaporates water from these water bodies which form water vapor and rise with air to form clouds, thereby forming the water cycle.

Ocean Currents

Answer the following questions.

1. There are five major ocean gyres on Earth. Draw arrows along each of the circles to indicate the direction of currents in the ocean.

2. The following are the names of the gyres. Label them correctly on the map.

➢ North Atlantic Gyre   ➢ North Pacific Gyre

➢ South Pacific Gyre   ➢ Indian Ocean Gyre

➢ South Atlantic Gyre

3. What are the two types of ocean currents?

4. How are these ocean currents driven?

Greenhouse Effect

1. How does the Earth's surface receive and lose heat energy?

   _____

   _____

2. An increased amount of greenhouse gases will hamper the loss of heat energy from the Earth's surface. Imagine that the amount of greenhouse gases at the equator is 10 times more than the normal.

   a. How does this affect the water expansion in that region?

   _____

   _____

   _____

   _____

   b. How will the following be impacted due to the increased amount of greenhouse gases?

   i. Surface currents

   ii. Water levels

   iii. Temperature

   _____

   _____

Climate vs Weather

1. How is weather different from climate?

Climate	Weather

2. Given below are climatic and weather conditions of five different states in the USA. Make a table distinguishing the climatic conditions from weather conditions of each state.

a. Summer in Texas lasts from June to August with a temperature ranging between 86°F and 98°F. The temperature on 26th July 2019 was 90°F with wind blowing at 15 mph. Winter lasts from December to February with a temperature ranging between 45°F and 65°F. On Christmas day, 2019 the temperature was 18°C during the day and 6°C during the night.

b. Winter lasts from December to January in Arizona where January is the coldest month. Night temperatures are below freezing in northern and central parts but are mild in the south and west. Hawley Lake in Arizona recorded the coldest temperature of -40°C on January 7, 1971.

c. The hottest months in New Jersey are from June to August with temperatures ranging from 77°F to 87°F. The temperature in winter ranges from 49.2°F to 38°F. New Jersey recorded a humidity of 86% and temperature of 11°C on 9th April 2020.

d. Autumn in Illinois is from mid October to November with average day temperature ranging from 15.6°C to 21.1°C and night temperature ranging from 4.4°C to 10°C. The wind blew at a speed of 21 mph on 8th April 2020 and recorded a temperature of 6°C at 10 am.

Name of the state	Weather Conditions	Climatic Conditions

Name of the state	Weather Conditions	Climatic Conditions

Name of the state	Weather Conditions	Climatic Conditions

Name of the state	Weather Conditions	Climatic Conditions

Convection in the Mantle

Imagine you are Hot blob in the Earth's mantle. Mark your position as Hot Blob in the image given. Describe your journey in the lower mantle. Use the word 'convection' in your description.

_____

_____

_____

_____

_____

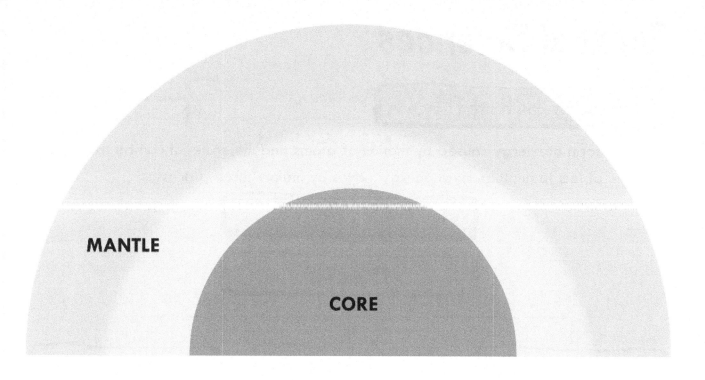

Your friend is Cool Blob in the Earth's mantle. Mark the position of Cool Blob in the image given. In the convection process, where can you find your friend with respect to the lithosphere? Will you ever meet your friend?

Physical Sciences

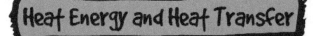
Heat Energy and Heat Transfer

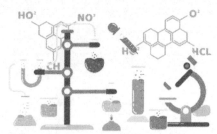

Heat is a form of energy caused by motion of atoms and molecules. It can be transferred from one object to another. Heat energy moves by mainly three processes.

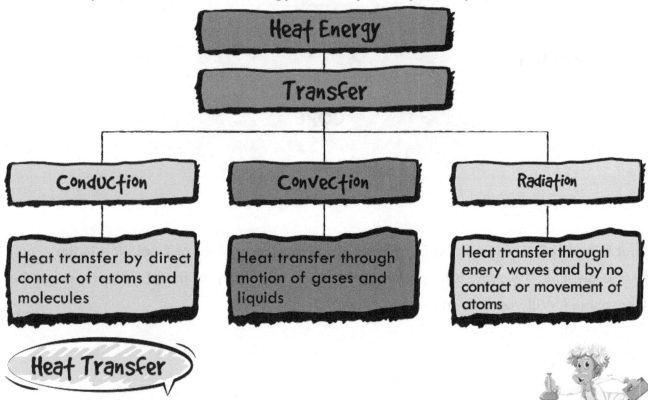

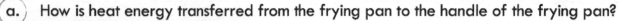
Heat Transfer

Identify the ways in which heat energy has been transferred in the following. Choose the correct answer.

a. How is heat energy transferred from the frying pan to the handle of the frying pan?

☐ Conduction

☐ Convection

☐ Radiation

www.prepaze.com

212

prepaze

b. How does the heat from the fireplace get transferred to the hands?

- [ ] Conduction
- [ ] Convection
- [ ] Radiation

c. How does the heat from the kettle transfer to the water inside it?

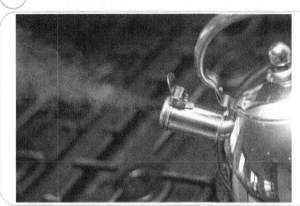

- [ ] Conduction
- [ ] Convection
- [ ] Radiation

Testing Heat Transfer

Perform the following in the presence of an adult at home. Switch on the cooking hob in your kitchen. Wait for five minutes. Place your hand one foot above the hob that has been turned on.

1. Did you feel warm air against your palm?

    ☐ Yes

    ☐ No

2. How did the heat from the hot hob get transferred to your hand? Name the method of heat transfer.

_____

_____

_____

_____

Activity for Heat Transfer

Perform the following activity with the help of an adult.

Place a glass of water in the refrigerator for 30 minutes. Then, boil some water in a kettle. Pour the hot water from the kettle into a vessel and place the glass of cold water immersed inside that vessel. Your setup will look something similar to the image given below.

Activity Setup

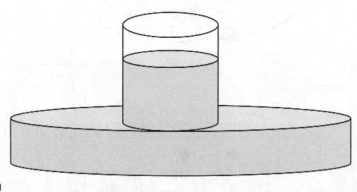

After 10 minutes, dip your finger into the glass of water (placed inside the vessel) and note down what you observed in the space below.

Observation

_____

_____

_____

_____

_____

Which of the following statements hold true for the above experiment? Choose the correct statements.

☐ Heat from the glass of water gets transferred to the water in the vessel.

☐ Heat from the kettle gets transferred to the water in it by radiation.

☐ Heat moves from cooler regions to warmer regions.

☐ Heat from the kettle gets transferred to the water in it by convection.

☐ Heat from the hot water in the vessel gets transferred to the glass by conduction.

☐ Heat moves from warmer regions to cooler regions.

Heat Transfer through Materials

Plastic, wood, metal - which of these materials is best suited for making kitchen utensils like saucepans. Why?

Describe the method of heat transfer that helps in cooking food.

Modes of Heat Transfer

Identify the modes of heat transfer for the following activities to happen and define them.

1.

Hair dryer at a salon

Heat transfer by _____

Definition:

_____
_____
_____

2.

Food cooked on a pan

Heat transfer by _____

Definition:

_____
_____
_____

3.

Ice cream melting in the sun

Heat transfer by _____

Definition:

_____
_____
_____

www.prepaze.com

Life Sciences - Ecology

Energy Flow in Living Things

A group of living things and their physical surroundings together can be defined as an ecosystem. Not all living organisms in an ecosystem can make their own food. Sun's energy is trapped by plants in an ecosystem in the process of photosynthesis. They use water, sunlight, and air to process their own food for energy. For this reason, plants are called the producers. Plants in turn are consumed by animals. Living things that cannot make their own food but depend on other living organisms for food are called consumers. All animals are consumers.

Consumers can be classified into different types based on what they consume.

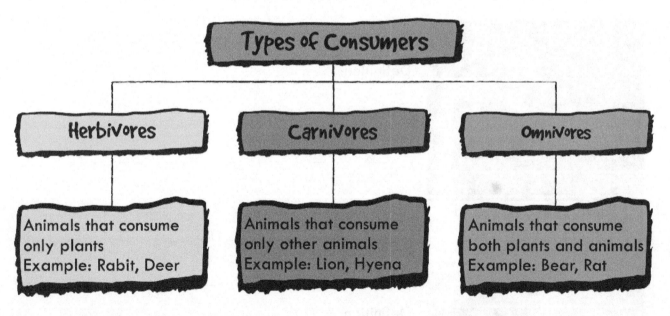

Producers and consumers together form a food chain, where each living thing is dependent on another living thing for food and energy. Many such food chains co-exists in an ecosystem. Sometimes, a living thing in one food chain becomes a source of food for living things in two or more food chains. Such interconnected and interdependent food chains are known as food webs.

www.prepaze.com

Ecosystem and Its Factors

1. Mention the living and nonliving things in the ecosystem presented above.

Living Things	Nonliving Things

2. Mention the producers and consumers in this ecosystem. Draw or write one food chain that you see.

Producers	Consumers

3. What might happen if the sun stops shining in this ecosystem? Mention the changes that will happen.

_____

_____

_____

_____

_____

4. What will happen if there is no rainfall for several months here? Mention the changes that will happen.

_____

_____

_____

_____

_____

5. Explain what might happen if the number of hawks increased in number. Mention the changes that will happen.

_____

_____

_____

6. What will happen if waste water from an industry mixes with the water in this ecosystem?

_____

_____

_____

_____

7. Write three other changes that might occur in this ecosystem and effects that they will have.

	Change	Effect on the Ecosystem
1.		
2.		
3.		

Producers and Consumers

Hannah has a vegetable garden. In the garden, there are bees sucking nectar from flowers and birds pecking seeds from the ground. Hannah harvests her daily dose of greens from her own garden.

1. Identify the producers and consumers from the above scenario and list them below.

Producers	Consumers

2. Name three other producers and consumers you see in your environment.

_____

_____

_____

_____

Food Chains and Food Webs

Observe the given images and answer the questions that follow.

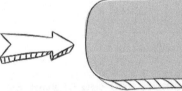

1. How many food chains do you see? Write the food chains as shown in the template below.

(Hint: To make a food chain you need to connect at least three living things that depend on other organisms for food)

2. What is a food web?

_____

_____

_____

_____

3. Can the organisms in the pictures given above form a food web?

☐ Yes

☐ No

4. Draw a food web with these organisms and label it.

5. Which among the given living things is the following?

Herbivore: _____

Carnivore: _____

Omnivore: _____

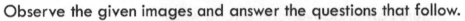

Energy Flow in Food Webs

Observe the given images and answer the questions that follow.

1. How do these living things form a food chain? Write it in the food chain template given below.

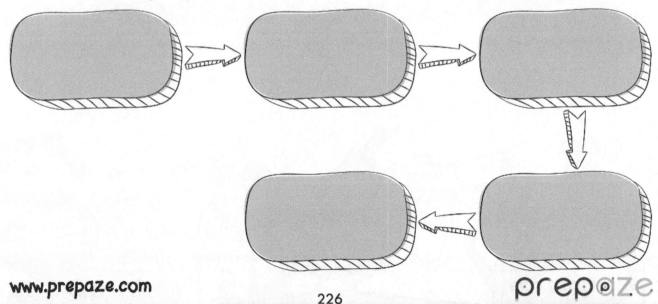

2. How do these living things arrange themselves in an energy pyramid? Why?

Relationships Between Organisms

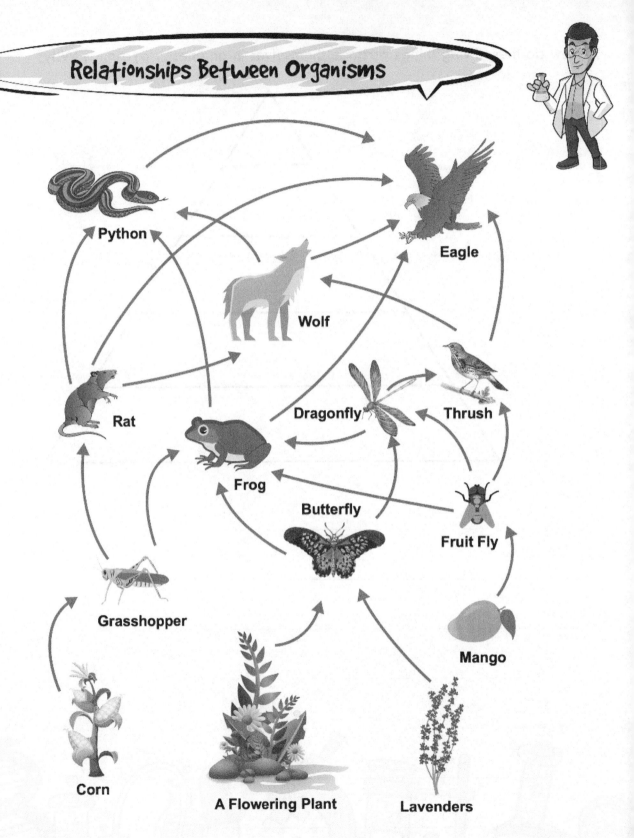

Study the food web given above and answer the questions given.

1. Identify and write five food chains from the food web given.

Food Chain 1

Food Chain 2

Food Chain 3

Food Chain 4

Food Chain 5

2. Identify and write the following from the food web:

a. 3 producers:

_____

_____

b. 5 consumers:

_____

_____

_____

3. How do the producers obtain energy? Choose one food chain and describe the energy flow in it.

_____

_____

_____

_____

4. Consider the rat, python, and eagle in the food web above. Choose the relevant options for each of the following questions.

a. What is the relation between the python and the eagle?

☐ Competition

☐ Predator/Prey

☐ Symbiosis

b. What is the relation between the rat and the eagle?

- [ ] Competition
- [ ] Predator/Prey
- [ ] Symbiosis

c. What is the relation between the rat and the python?

- [ ] Competition
- [ ] Predator/Prey
- [ ] Symbiosis

5. Refer to the food web and name two animals that have the following relations. Give two examples each.

Competition:

_____

Predator/Prey:

_____

6. In the given food web, where will you place the eagle and the plants in the energy pyramid. Why?

_____

_____

_____

Animals and Adaptations

Climates vary across different regions. These determine the type of vegetation and animals that thrive in different regions. Places with distinct climates with particular plant and animal communities are called biomes. There are six major biomes across the world.

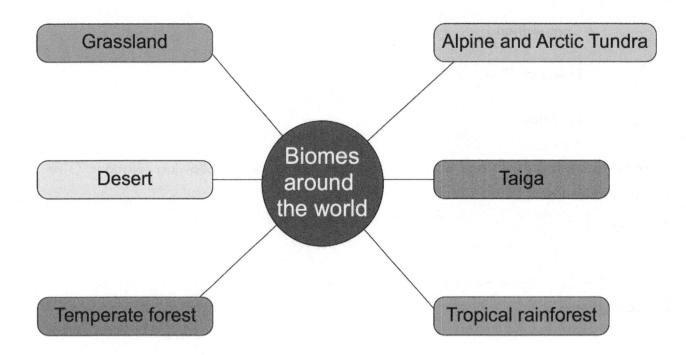

Plants and animals living in these different biomes develop different adaptations to survive the climatic conditions. For example: Spider monkeys in the tropical rainforests have long tails and arms to move across trees. Tropical rainforests are dense with vegetation with constant rain. Grasslands are places that have too little rainfall for forests. These places often have wildfires. Animals living in these regions are adapted to live here. Animals such as wildebeest in grasslands have long legs to escape and run away from fires. Smaller animals make burrows and hide from fires.

Reason behind Adaptations

1. A spider monkey in the rainforests has long and strong limbs to climb trees. What adaptations do you think a monkey would have to survive in the tundra region? Why?

___
___
___
___
___
___

2. A Fennec fox lives in the Sahara. It has nocturnal habits which helps it deal with searing heat of the desert environment. It has physical adaptations such as distinctive batlike ears. It helps the fox radiate heat and keep the body cool. It has thick long hair that insulates it during cold nights and protects it from hot sun.

What adaptations would you want to develop to survive in the tropical rainforest? Why?

Regions and Adaptations

Identify the biomes where the specified adaptations are needed by the organisms that live there. Also provide one example organism for each of the adaptations.

Adaptation	Biome	Organism
Specially adapted toes for walking on sand		
Hollow stem to store water		
Thick fur to keep warm		
Strong teeth and claws		
Ability to change color to avoid predators		
Long eyelashes to protect eyes from sandstorm		
Hump where fat and water can be stored		

Leaves are modified to thorns to avoid loss of water		
Nostrils on top of the head		
Long, deep roots		
Eyes on top of the head		
Webbed feet		

Who am I?

Use the clues about adaptations to identify the organism. Also write what will happen if the organism loses that adaptation.

1. I only eat leaves from eucalyptus trees. I also eat dirt and rocks to ease my digestion.

_____

_____

_____

2. I taste the air with my tongue. That helps me follow my prey.

_____

_____

_____

3. My tusks help me dig underground water.

_____

_____

_____

4. I go up and down the mountains without care. I find my food here where others wouldn't dare.

_____

_____

_____

5. I have a long sticky tongue but no teeth. I dig up using my sharp claws and feed on insects from underneath.

6. I drink water that is recycled from the moisture in my breath. I have to do this, or I die.

7. Getting food is a breeze for a swimmer like me. I can hunt deep underwater for a long time despite the sub-zero climate.

Resources

Types of Resources

Resources based on utility, availability, distribution, and time required for their formation can be classified into two major types - renewable and non-renewable resources.

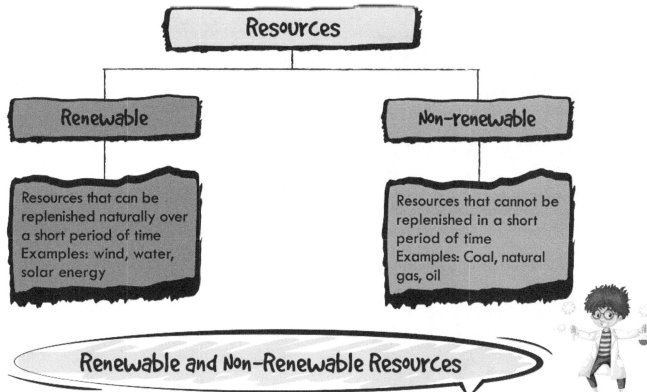

Renewable and Non-Renewable Resources

Observe the different pictures given below. Identify and name the resources used in each of the pictures. Classify them as either renewable or non-renewable by choosing the correct option.

1.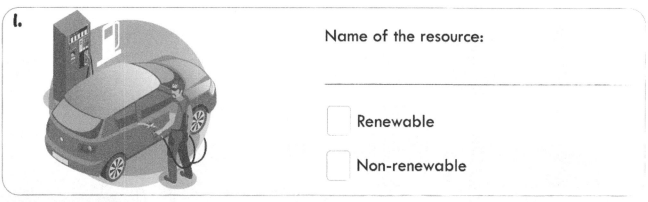

Name of the resource:

_____

☐ Renewable

☐ Non-renewable

2.

Name of the resource:

_____

☐ Renewable

☐ Non-renewable

3.

Name of the resource:

_____

☐ Renewable

☐ Non-renewable

4.

Name of the resource:

_____

☐ Renewable

☐ Non-renewable

5.

Name of the resource:

_____

☐ Renewable

☐ Non-renewable

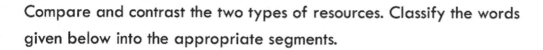

Compare and Contrast

Compare and contrast the two types of resources. Classify the words given below into the appropriate segments.

- coal
- fossil fuels
- energy resource
- can be replenished
- natural gas
- cannot be replenished
- can produce electricity
- cannot produce electricity
- water
- oil
- cause pollution
- wind
- sunlight
- wood
- do not cause pollution

Renewable Resources	Common Attributes	Non Renewable Resources

Complete the given sentences and identify the answers in the word grid.

1. A renewable energy source that is available in plenty and allows us to breathe is _____.

2. A resource that can be replenished is said to be _____.

3. A resource that cannot be replenished is said to be _____.

4. The energy resource that is formed over millions of years and cannot be replenished is _____.

5. The resource used to burn and obtain electricity is _____.

6. Uranium is used in the making of _____ energy.

7. Wood or corn make the _____ from which fuels are made.

8. _____ is another name for oil.

9. A nonrenewable resource which is pumped out from pockets both onshore and offshore is _____.

10. _____ is obtained from the Sun.

E	U	B	N	I	X	I	O	I	R	Q	F	D
R	N	P	O	M	C	J	L	U	G	P	O	V
T	H	E	N	U	C	L	E	A	R	K	S	S
C	V	T	R	M	N	M	A	Y	H	C	S	A
Y	G	R	E	N	E	R	A	L	O	S	I	G
B	R	O	N	N	A	N	D	S	I	I	L	L
J	N	L	E	E	D	B	F	S	I	H	F	A
K	I	E	W	O	F	J	I	A	O	G	U	R
H	Q	U	A	R	G	D	J	M	L	F	E	U
Y	W	M	B	T	S	N	C	O	A	L	L	T
R	E	N	L	P	A	I	K	I	Z	S	S	A
I	K	R	E	N	E	W	A	B	L	E	O	N

Biomes That We Live In

Henry lives in a tropical country. The following are the climatic conditions that prevail throughout the year.

March to August	Summer, sunny with temperature ranging from 35°C to 40°C with strong breeze in the months of July and August
September to November	Rainy
December to February	Winter, mostly cloudy with very little sun

1. List down the electrical appliances that are essential for Henry at home.

_____

_____

_____

_____

2. Among the listed appliances, which of the electrical appliances need to be working everyday?

_____

_____

_____

_____

3. What can you say about the energy consumption at Henry's house?

☐ High

☐ Low

4. Given the climatic conditions:

a. What kinds of energy sources are suitable to obtain electricity in the long run?

☐ Renewable

☐ Non-renewable

Why?

_____
_____
_____

b. Mention two energy resources that will be useful to obtain electricity.

_____
_____
_____

c. Mention the months in which they will be the most useful. Why?

_____
_____
_____

Energy Scavenger Hunt

Use the Internet to find answers to the following questions.

1. What are fossil fuels?
   _____
   _____
   _____
   _____

2. What are renewable energy sources? Give three examples.
   _____
   _____
   _____
   _____

3. What types of gases make up natural gas?
   _____
   _____
   _____
   _____

4. What percent of the world's electricity is supplied by hydropower?
   _____

5. What is nuclear energy?

_____
_____
_____

6. By what percentage is the use of wind power growing worldwide each year?

_____

7. How did oil and natural gas form?

_____
_____
_____

8. What percentage of electricity is powered by solar energy worldwide?

_____

Creative Writing

Imagine the world has run out of non-renewable resources. What would the world be like? Draw and describe in your words. Also include points about how your everyday life will be affected/different from how it is today.

Conservation of Natural Resources

Imagine yourself facing the following problems. Suggest solutions for the same.

What would you do if you see many sheets of paper with only one side used going to the trash?

What would you do if you see the Earth's temperature rising due to global warming?

What would you do if you see a lot of plastic bottles, aluminium cans, and cardboards piling up at your home?

What would you do if you see prices of fuel getting higher and higher?

What would you do if you see a newly born monkey lying on a trail?

What would you do if you see the rainforest disappearing?

What would you do if you see a running tap in the wash when you are brushing your teeth?

What would you do if you see people hunting animals?

_____
_____
_____

What would you do if you see climate getting worse and more natural disasters occurring frequently?

_____
_____
_____

What would you do if you see some noisy youth camping and throwing away garbage?

_____
_____
_____

Vocabulary Check

Unscramble the following to make words that pertain to conservation of resources.

1. urensuscoretaar - _____

2. iticontbnuro - _____

3. aoosevrticnn - _____

4. oenleenwnabr - _____

5. iblgaomraingw - _____

6. souniotl - _____

7. issataebnlu - _____

8. ecelcyr - _____

9. ifussleisof - _____

10. eoaryenslgr - _____

11. sreue - _____

12. ncateligahcme - _____

13. oltipolnu - _____

14. esoeunsehgrag - _____

15. rweablnee - _____

Answers

English Answer Key

1. he

Explanation: None of us is more knowledgeable than he (is).

2. us

Explanation: The blank space requires an object. Hence the objective case "us" is the correct answer.

3. she

Explanation: The blank space requires a subject. Hence the subjective case "she" is the correct answer.

4. our

Explanation: The possessive case "our" answers the question "whose car was taken?"

5. your

Explanation: The possessive case "your" answers the question "whose arrival was appreciated?"

6. them

Explanation: The pronoun "them" has to be in the objective case. The pronoun "us" can be used as a clue.

Choose the correct pronoun case.

1. Whom should I trust?

Explanation: The objective case "whom" is required.

2. Is he the one for whom the remark is intended?

Explanation: The objective case "whom" is required.

3. He is the one who solved the crime.

Explanation: The subjective case "who" is required.

4. Who invited the parents?

Explanation: The subjective case "who" is required.

5. The celebrity whom we met was generous.

Explanation: The objective case "whom" is required.

Write YES against the sentences with the correct pronoun case, and NO against the sentences with incorrect pronoun case.

1. YES

Explanation: "She" completes the subject of the sentence. Hence the subjective case is correctly used.

2. NO

Explanation: The subject pronoun "we" is required.

3. YES

Explanation: I am as brave as she (is).

4. NO

Explanation: The objective case "him and her" should be used.

5. NO

Explanation: The objective case "whom" should be used instead of who.

6. NO

Explanation: The objective case "me" should be used instead of "I."

7. NO

Explanation: The subjective case "I" should be used in the subject place.

8. YES

Explanation: Who is the correct pronoun case as it is the subject of the clause "who has a student loan."

Correct the pronoun errors in the following sentences. Write NC against sentences with No Changes.

1. He joined **her** at the mall.

2. Jose and **I** were invited to the dance.

3. She is smarter than **I**.

4. **NC**

5. I noticed that it was **they** who started the work.

Intensive Pronouns

Complete Me

Use the appropriate intensive pronoun to complete each sentence.

1. himself
2. itself
3. herself
4. themselves
5. ourselves

Shift in Pronoun

Identify Pronoun Shift

1. B
Explanation: "You" is in second person, but "people" is in third person.

2. No change
Explanation: The sentence has no shift in pronoun.

3. C
Explanation: The correct pronoun is "they" for the antecedent artists.

4. No change
Explanation: The sentence has no shift in pronoun.

5. No change
Explanation: The sentence has no shift in pronoun.

Vague Pronoun

Fix Me

1. After completing the work, Tom went to congratulate Harry.
Explanation: It's vague to whom the pronoun "he" refers. There are more than one antecedent.

2. Rosa told Jenny, "The principal advised me not to cut class."
Explanation: It's vague to whom the pronoun "her" refers. There are more than one antecedent.

3. The library and the bookshop are closing. We already miss reading the books.
Explanation: It's vague to what the pronoun "them" refers. The antecedent is missing.

4. Mom told Christy, "I'm going to watch my favorite movie."

Explanation: It's vague to whom the pronoun "her" refers. There are more than one antecedent.

1. Incorrect

Explanation: The intensive pronoun themselves should replace ourselves since the speaker is not in the action, but his/her parents are.

2. Correct

Explanation: The possessive pronoun my and the noun employees are correctly used.

3. Incorrect

Explanation: The pronoun "yours" should replace your to show possession.

4. Incorrect

Explanation: The objective case "me" is required here.

5. Correct

Explanation: The subjective case "I" is correctly used in the compound subject.

6. Incorrect

Explanation: The pronoun "she" is vague, it's not clear if she refers to Charlotte or Isabella.

Identify the sentence with the correct punctuation marks.

1. a

Explanation: "Alaska" is a parenthetical element in this sentence which needs to be set off with a pair of commas.

2. c

Explanation: "in Greek Legend" is the parenthetical element in this sentence.

3. c

Explanation: "In 2005" is an introductory phrase and "Illinois" is a parenthetical element in this sentence.

4. c

Explanation: " who was an English poet, playwright, and actor" is the nonrestrictive clause/parenthetical element in this sentence.

5. b

Explanation: "in my opinion" is the parenthetical element in this sentence.

6. c

Explanation: "as you will see" is the parenthetical element in this sentence.

Punctuate Me

Add commas, dashes, or parentheses to fix the below sentences.

We do not recommend that, no.
Explanation: "no" is the parenthetical element (interjection) in this sentence.

Take — for example — the way he runs his office; it is a testimony of his loyalty.
Explanation: " for example " is the parenthetical element in this sentence.

The warnings, however, did not have an effect.
Explanation: "however" is the parenthetical element in this sentence.

A few people (who I won't name) don't appreciate what they have.
Explanation: " who I won't name " is the parenthetical element in this sentence.

Spelling

Word Scramble

Rearrange the letters to find the words.

PRECURSORS   ELABORATE

PRIORITY   DRASTIC

ARTIFACT   RETRIEVE

Untangle Me

Follow the lines and rearrange the letters. Write the correct word in the boxes.

elephant   starfish

pumpkin   eggplant

strawberry

Secret Word

Figure out the secret word.

C R Y P T O G R A P H Y

Word Puzzle

www.prepaze.com

Sentence Pattern

Add the Object

Each of the below sentences has a subject followed by a verb. Use the appropriate object to complete each sentence.

1. tennis
2. pizza
3. room
4. hole
5. salad

Find the Pair

Identify the sentence pattern and match accordingly.

1. S+V+O

Explanation: I / met / them. "Them" is the object as it receives the action of the verb "met whom?"

2. S+V+A

Explanation: It / rained / today. "Today" is an adverbial in this sentence as it answers "when" it rained.

3. S+V+O+C

Explanation: This / makes / me / happy. "Me" is the object and "happy" is the complement.

4. S+V+IO+DO

Explanation: The nurse / gave / her / an injection. "Her" is the indirect object to whom the injection was given. "An injection" is the direct object that receives the action of the verb "what was given?"

5. V+O

Explanation: Call / him. This is one of the sentence patterns without a subject; the implied subject here is "you." The sentence has only a verb and an object "him" (who is to be called).

6. S+V+C

Explanation: They / seem / anxious. "Anxious" is the complement that explains how "they seem" and completes the sentence.

Jumbled Sentences

1. Her father is a mechanic. S+V+C

2. Yesterday, they ran. A+S+V

3. He got his ears pierced. S+V+O+C

4. They sold us their car. S+V+IO+DO

5. I wrote a poem. S+V+O

6. Jose lost his wallet with his license in the subway. S+V+O+C+A

This or That?

Choose the pattern of the given sentences.

1. S+V+IO+DO

Explanation: My mother (S) gave (V) me (IO) a present (DO).

2. S+V+O+A

Explanation: She (S) sent (V) a postcard (O) from Rome (A).

3. S+V+C+A

Explanation: You (S) seem (V) upset (C) today (A).

4. S+V+O

Explanation: My uncle's friend (S) raised (V) a wild animal (O).

5. S+V+O+C+A

Explanation: I (S) took (V) my pet, wounded (C) to the vet (A).

Identify the Pattern

Read the sentences and write the pattern in the given boxes.

1. VO

Explanation: Excuse (V) me (O).

2. SVCA

Explanation: It (S) is (V) dirty (C) here (A).

3. SVOA

Explanation: They (S) sold (V) the house (O) last year (A).

4. SVC

Explanation: The children (S) were (V) tired (C).

Context Clues

What is the Meaning?

Find the meaning of the underlined words using the clues.

1. a

Explanation: The words "many friends" in the sentence indicates that she was a friendly person.

2. c

Explanation: The word "painful" indicates that the preceding word is also a negative word. Choices a and b are positive words.

3. b

Explanation: The words "multiple stops to rest and refresh" indicates that the journey must be tiring.

4. c

Explanation: The words "speaker to hear it clearly" indicates that the speech was unhearable.

5. b

Explanation: The words "surrounding and could not win" indicates that the word means to surrender.

Add Prefixes

For the following words, add the appropriate prefixes to form their opposites.

misunderstand	misbehave
disconnect	disagree
misinterpret	unacceptable
disclose	disengage

Match the words with the appropriate suffixes.

1. conformist
2. manageable
3. running
4. defensible
5. wishful
6. awareness

Use a Dictionary

Find the meaning of the following words and use them in a sentence.

Answers may vary

disparage	belittle
galvanizing	shock or excite
ramify	branch
adversarial	involving opposition
undulate	a wavy pattern
deliberate	careful consideration

Find the various synonyms for the following words.

Answers may vary

This dress fits like a glove. - simile

Explanation: The fitting of a dress and glove is compared.

The room is exactly as she described. - not a simile

Explanation: There is no comparison between the two objects "room" and "she."

She is brave as a lion. - simile

Explanation: The bravery of a person and a lion is compared.

My siblings fight like cats and dogs. - simile

Explanation: The fighting of the siblings and cats and dogs is compared.

He missed the beginning as he was late. - not a simile

Explanation: There is no comparison between the two objects "he" and "beginning."

They looked as if they were lost. - not a simile

Explanation: There is only one object "they," and there is no comparison.

The horse ran like the wind. - simile

Explanation: The speed of a horse and the wind is compared.

Answers may vary

1. She sings like a bird.

2. He is as proud as a peacock.

3. I slept like a log.

4. The camp was as safe as a house.

5. They are as different as night and day.

Write YES for sentences with metaphors and NO for sentences without a metaphor.

They are guarding the house. - NO

Explanation: There is no comparison between the two things "they" and "house."

Ashley is an angel. - YES

Explanation: The implied comparison is that Ashley is good and kind as an angel.

My parents believe me. - NO

Explanation: There is no comparison between the two things "parents" and "me."

He is my biggest admirer. - NO

Explanation: The admirer is compared with other admirers, but there is no comparison between the two things "he" and "admirer."

She is a tiger. - YES

Explanation: The implied comparison is that she is fierce as a tiger.

Eden is a teacher. NO
Explanation: There is no comparison between the two objects "Eden" and "teacher."

Ann broke into the conversation. - YES
Explanation: The implied comparison is that Ann broke into the conversation as a burglar breaks into a house.

What Is the Quality?

Find the quality that is compared in these metaphors. Explain the comparison in the space provided.

1. heat
Explanation: The heat of the place is compared to an oven.

2. movement
Explanation: Like birds, children moved together in a crowd to see the show.

3. shine/brightness
Explanation: She shines or outperforms others as a star.

4. getting somewhere before others
Explanation: Lee usually arrives or acts before others

5. events/actors
Explanation: The people and events in the world are compared to the actors and stories in plays.

Sort Me

Categorize the below statements. Write the serial numbers in the respective circle.

The child is afraid of darkness. (neither)
Explanation: There is no comparison between the two objects "child" and "darkness."

They are watching us like a hawk. (simile)
Explanation: They are watching us very closely as a hawk watches its prey.

She watched as the train left. (neither)
Explanation: There is no comparison between the two objects "she" and "train."

The relationship turned sour. (metaphor)
Explanation: The relationship is compared to sour taste to imply that it is no longer satisfactory.

The bannister is as cold as ice. (simile)
Explanation: The bannister is compared to ice.

Books are better than movies. (neither)
Explanation: This is a direct comparison. Metaphor uses indirect comparison, and this cannot be a simile as the words "like/as" are not used.

My brother is a rock. (metaphor)
Explanation: The strength or reliability of the brother is compared to a rock.

The kettle was as black as coal. (simile)
Explanation: The color of the kettle and coal is compared.

Riddle

Ans: Queue/Q

Personification and Hyperbole

Personification or Hyperbole?

Read the sentences and choose the correct answer.

1. Personification
Explanation: The leaves are given a human quality "dance."

2. Hyperbole
Explanation: "Ton" is an exaggeration to mean that the bag was heavy.

3. Hyperbole
Explanation: "A million times" is an exaggeration used to imply that something was told many times.

4. Personification
Explanation: "Sleep" is a human quality, which is attributed to a city in this sentence.

5. Hyperbole
Explanation: "To the moon and back" is an exaggerated way to express love.

6. Personification
Explanation: "Anger" and "devour" are human qualities attributed to the fierce storm.

Word Analogies

Complete the Analogy

Find the relationship between the first pair of words. Then complete the second pair using the same relationship.

1. a
Explanation: The relationship is "object:description."

2. d
Explanation: The relationship is "synonym."

3. c

Explanation: The relationship is "part to whole."

4. b

Explanation: The relationship is "object:exterior protection."

5. c

Explanation: The relationship is "antonym."

Find the Relationship

Select the choice that best describes the relationship between the word pairs.

1. b

Explanation: The relationship is object and classification. Beaver is a rodent and shirt is a type of clothing.

2. d

Explanation: The relationship is object and function. Microscope is used to magnify and lighthouse is used to warn us.

3. c

Explanation: The relationship is part to whole. Sector is a part of a circle and entry is a part of a dictionary.

4. d

Explanation: The relationship is performer to action. A teacher educates as an author writes

Connotation and Denotation

Neutral, Positive, or Negative?

Identify the connotation of the underlined words.

1. negative
2. positive
3. negative
4. neutral
5. positive

Complete the Fish

Write the positive words from the list on the upper side of the fishbone and write the synonymous negative words on the other side.

Positive	Negative
aroma	stench
energetic	hyperactive
assertive	pushy

www.prepaze.com

Reading: Literature

The Beetle

Story Analysis

1. b
Explanation: The beetle is the story's title character.

2. c
Explanation: The beetle left as it felt the horse was treated better than he was.

3. b
Explanation: The beetle found the frogs on the linen.

4. a
Explanation: The lady-bird finds the garden beautiful, but the beetle does not agree as it finds dung-heap to be better than the garden.

5. a
Explanation: The beetle thinks too much of itself and is unable to adapt.

6. c
Explanation: The beetle would have lost its life if the girls had not freed it.

7. c
Explanation: The writer shows understanding of the thoughts of all the characters in the story. Hence, it is third person omniscient.

8. a
Explanation: In the end, the beetle returned to the stable from where it started its journey.

9. c
Explanation: The beetle in the end tries to use the situation to its advantage by realizing that it can ride the horse instead of wanting the golden shoes.

10. c
Explanation: Just as the beetle, we often don't realize what we have and are unappreciative. Also, being envious of others' success is not constructive.

Character Analysis

horse - loyal

beetle - conceited

caterpillar - optimistic

gardener's son - atrocious

fly - inconsiderate

girls - helpful

ladybugs - appreciative

Arrange the following in the order in which they are introduced in the story.

1. HORSE   5. EARWIGS

2. BEETLE   6. BOY

3. CATERPILLAR 7. FLY

4. FROGS   8. GIRLS

Pirate Story

Section A

1. adventure

Explanation: The poem is about the children pretending to go on a voyage adventure.

2. sea

Explanation: The phrase afloat in the meadow indicates that the children were pretending that the meadow was the sea in which their vessel was afloat.

3. abab

Explanation: swing and spring rhyme; lea and sea rhyme.

Three of us afloat in the meadow by the swing,(a)

Three of us abroad in the basket on the lea. (b)

Winds are in the air, they are blowing in the spring, (a)

And waves are on the meadow like the waves there are at sea.(b)

4. first person

Explanation: The narrator is part of the story, hence uses "us" and "we."

5. enthusiastic

Explanation: The narrator is excited with friends in planning the adventure.

6. metaphor

Explanation: The cattle charging is a metaphor to how they imagine the squadron is approaching them.

Section B

1. afloat - boat; star- Malabar

Explanation: They have the same ending sound.

2. Any of these is an acceptable answer: cattle is a metaphor for squadron; wicket is a metaphor for harbor; garden is a metaphor for shore.

Explanation: These are metaphors as they share a common quality.

3. undecided

Explanation: They are undecided as they were escaping the squadron before they decided if they are venturing toward Africa, Providence, Babylon, or Malabar.

Connecting to Text

Answer may vary

Match the Metaphors

meadow - sea

basket - ship

grass - waves

children - pirates

wicket - harbor

garden - shore

The Moon

Comparing Texts

Section A

1. nightlife and moon

2. influence and relationship between the earth and moon

3. to entertain

4. to inform

5. third person

6. unproved idea or theory

7. simile

8. personification: the flowers are personified as humans by giving them human quality "closing eyes."

9. The moon was formed after the earth was formed.

10. The moon shines on everything that is out in the night.

Section B

1. Similarity: Both talk about the moon and earth.

2. Difference: The passage talks about the moon in the perspective of science, whereas the poem talks about the moon in the perspective of the author.

3. The passage requires more research and scientific facts.

Answer may vary

Reading: Informational Text

The Founding Fathers of the USA

1. The founding fathers are George Washington, Alexander Hamilton, Benjamin Franklin, John Adams, Samuel Adams, Thomas Jefferson, James Madison, and John Jay.

2. James Madison

3. George Washington

4. First – George Washington, Second – John Adams, Third – Thomas Jefferson, Fourth – James Madison

5. Thomas Jefferson and James Madison

6. John Jay

7. Benjamin Franklin

Identify the hidden words using the clues given below:

A	V	U	B	D	O	J	T	O	C	W	F
C	B	I	E	J	V	E	M	Y	R	B	J
D	T	C	N	O	A	F	W	A	X	U	N
E	Q	T	I	H	T	F	R	L	A	I	Z
R	S	G	D	N	Z	E	L	J	K	Y	G
A	Q	M	C	J	E	R	E	H	S	V	P
Q	T	P	F	A	Y	S	F	N	O	Z	X
X	L	H	O	Y	G	O	S	G	K	L	A
Q	S	P	K	Z	N	N	D	I	H	B	W
N	O	T	G	N	I	H	S	A	W	I	V
B	J	O	H	N	A	D	A	M	S	X	J
G	R	F	J	Y	F	R	I	L	C	K	W
J	A	M	E	S	M	A	D	I	S	O	N

Fill in the Blanks

1. Alexander Hamilton
2. 1789 to 1797.
3. 13
4. third
5. James Madison

Word Meaning

Find the meaning of the following words using a dictionary and the context.

Profession – A job or an occupation

President – Head of a country or a company

Constitution – A body of fundamental principles based on which a country or organization is governed

Independence – The state of being independent

Province – An administrative division of a country

Pet Survey

Interpretation of Data

1. 7%
2. 20%
3. birds
4. dogs
5. others
6. fish
7. 14%
8. 1%
9. dogs-cats-birds-others
10. birds-fish-cats-dogs

Data Transfer

Transfer the data from the graph to the below table.

	City	Countryside
Dogs	35%	21%
Cats	29%	20%
Fish	18%	18%
Birds	11%	12%
Others	7%	29%

Math Answer Key

Ratio And Proportional Relationships

1.

a. The ratio of Tulips: roses is 3:2

b. The ratio of Tulips: Total number of flowers is 3: 5

c. The ratio of Roses: Tulips is 2:3

Fruit Bowl Ratio

2.

a. The ratio of Oranges to strawberries is 3: 2. There are 3 oranges and 2 strawberries

b. The ratio of strawberries to oranges is 2: 3. There are 2 strawberries and 3 oranges.

c. The ratio of Oranges to the total number of fruits is 3: 5 There are totally 5 fruits of which 3 are oranges.

d. The ratio of Strawberries to the total number of fruits is 2: 5. There are 5 fruits, out of which 2 are strawberries.

Fun Project at Lego Corp

3.

a. Ratio of gray blocks to black blocks is 3:1

b. Ratio of gray blocks to the total number of blocks is 3:5

c. Ratio of black blocks to the total number of blocks is 2:5

4. Emi is correct. She has drawn 2 circles and 3 triangles.

How Many Stars and Moons?

5. There are 8 stars and 4 moons For Every 2 stars there is a moon. Hence the ratio of wrong answers to correct answers is 1: 2.

How Long Will Miss. Snail crawl?

6.

a. The ratio of distance covered by snail to time taken is 10 : 4.
   Therefore in 1 second it covers = 2.5 cm
   In 5 seconds it covers 5 x 2.5 = 12.5 cm

b. Time taken by the snail to cover 1 cm is = 0.4 sec
   Therefore to cover 20 cm it takes = 0.4 x 20 = 8 sec

7. The ratio between the number of apples and bottles of juice is 12 : 2

So, unit rate to make 1 bottle of juice is $\frac{12}{2}$ = 6.

Tom needs 6 apples to make 1 bottle of juice.

Amount of juice made with 1 apple = unit rate = $\frac{2}{12} = \frac{1}{6}$.

So, with 1 apple he can make $\frac{1}{6}$ th bottle of juice.

Number of apples	Bottles of apple juice produced
1	Unit rate is = $\frac{2}{12} = \frac{1}{6}$
3	3 x Unit rate to make juice with 3 apples = 3 x $\frac{1}{6} = \frac{1}{2}$
36	36 x Unit rate = 36 x $\frac{1}{6}$ = 6

8.

a. The unit rate $\dfrac{\text{people}}{\text{pizza}} = \dfrac{6}{3} = 2$ Therefore 1 pizza is for 2 people.

b. The unit rate $\dfrac{\text{people}}{\text{pizza}} = \dfrac{3}{6} = \dfrac{1}{2}$ Therefore each person gets $\dfrac{1}{2}$ pizza.

c. If there are 32 people attending the party he should order $32 \times \dfrac{1}{2} = 16$ pizzas

d. With 5 pizzas she can feed $5 \times 2 = 10$ people.

9. The ratio of snow : time $= \dfrac{1}{3} : 1$

Unit rate $= \dfrac{1}{\frac{1}{3}} = 3$. Therefore 1 inch of snow will fall in 3 hours.

For 6 inches of snow it will take $6 \times 3 = 18$ hours.

10. Unit rate is $\dfrac{1}{5}$ That is blue paint : yellow paint $= 1 : 5$.

One part of blue paint is mixed with 5 parts of yellow paint to obtain a shade of green.

So, Kim would need $10 \times 5 = 50$ pints of yellow paint.

11.

a) Ratio of flour to number of cupcakes is 3:10

Therefore unit rate $= \dfrac{3}{10}$

To make 20 cupcakes Ronnie needs $= 20 \times \dfrac{3}{10} = 6$ cups of 10 flour.

b) Ratio of flour to sugar is 3:2

Therefore unit rate is $\dfrac{3}{2}$

If Ronnie uses 4 cups of sugar, he would need $4 \times \dfrac{3}{2} = 6$ cups of flour.

Ratio of sugar to number of cupcakes is 2 : 10

Unit rate = $\dfrac{10}{2}$

Therefore 4 cups of sugar will yield = $\dfrac{10}{2} \times 4 = 20$ cupcakes

12.

	Apple	Orange	Glass of Juices
Original recipe	2	3	4
Double the recipe	2 x 2 = 4	3 x 2 = 6	4 x 2 = 8
Triple the recipe	2 x 3 = 6	3 x 3 = 9	4 x 3 = 12
Half the recipe	2 x ½ = 1	3 x 1/2 = 1 ½	4 x ½ = 2

13.

a. There are 100 small squares in the grid.

If 100 squares = $50, value of 1 small square = $\dfrac{50}{100} = \$\dfrac{1}{2}$

b. The grid has 100 small squares

If 100 squares = $200, Unit rate = 200/100 = $2

Value of 10 squares = $2 x 10 = $20

c. There are 100 small squares in the grid

If each small square = $2, value of the grid = $200

d. Value of 10 squares = $5

Value of 1 square = $\frac{5}{10} = 0.5$

There are 100 squares in the grid

Therefore, value of the grid = 0.5 x 100 = $50

14.

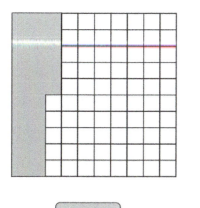 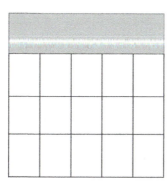 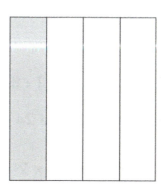

25/100   5/20   1/4

15.

a. $10\% = \frac{10}{100}$

$\frac{10}{100}$ of a number = 20

Therefore the number is $20 \times \frac{100}{10} = 200$

b. 25% of the number

$25\% = \frac{25}{100}$

Therefore the number is $\frac{25}{100} \times 200 = 50$

c. 5% of the number

$5\% = \frac{5}{100}$

Therefore the number is $\frac{5}{100} \times 200 = 10$

d. 200% of the number

$200\% = \dfrac{200}{100}$

Therefore the number is $\dfrac{200}{100} \times 200 = 400$

16.

a. The ratio of cups : ounce = 1 : 8 = 1 : 4

1 cup is 8 ounces, therefore 24 ounces = $\dfrac{24}{8}$ = 3 cups.

b. Ratio of ounce : quarts = 8 x 2 x 2 : 1 = 32 : 1

Therefore, 2 quarts = 32 x 2 = 64 ounces.

17.

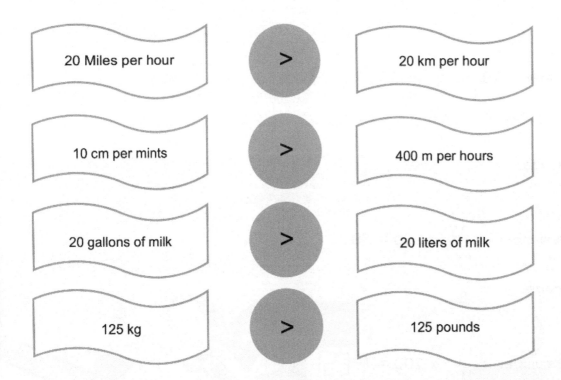

18.

Grid	Fraction	Percentage
a) (grid with 40 shaded)	40/100	40%
b) (grid with 35 shaded)	35/100	35%
c) (grid with 50 shaded)	50/100	50%

19.

a. 60% of the students are girls that is, 100 / 60

So, 18 girls are out of $\frac{100}{60} \times 18 = 30$ students.

Therefore, number of boys = 30 − 18 = 12

Ratio of number of boys to girls = $\frac{12}{18} = \frac{2}{3}$

b. Cost per head if 2 teachers accompanied the kids.

Total cost for the trip is transportation charges and refreshment charges

The bus travels 55 km one way, so total distance to cover is 55 + 55 = 110 km

Total transport charges = $5 x 110 = $550

Total refreshment charges = $250

Total amount spent = $550 + $250 = $800

18 girls + 12 boys + 2 teachers went for the picnic. Total = 32

Thus, cost per head = $\frac{800}{32}$ = $25

c. Out of 55 Km, 22 km is covered

Therefore percentage covered = $\frac{22}{55}$ x 100 = 40%

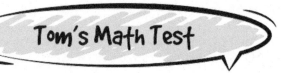

20.

a. 88 % = $\frac{88}{100}$. If he answered 22 of them correctly and got 88%, he wrote the test for 22 x $\frac{100}{88}$ = 25. Thus, he wrote the test for 25 marks.

b. To convert it to percentage multiply by 100, thus he scored $\frac{24}{25}$ x 100 = 96%

Number System

Kiara's Kitchen

1.

a. The Model represent decimal multiplication of 210 X 7.03

b.

				2	1	0
×				7 . 0	3
+				6	3	0
+			0	0	0	0
+		1	4	7	0	
=		1	4	7	6 . 3	0

Help Ryan Floor the Pool

2. Area of the pool = 70.25 X 5 = 351.25 sq. m
   Area of the tile = 10 cm X 10 cm = 100 sq. cm = 0.01 sq. m
   Number of tiles required to cover = 351.25 ÷ 0.01 = 35125 tiles.

Traffic Light Mystery

3. Find the LCM of 2 and 3 and add to the time, 7 am.
   LCM of 2,3 = 6
   They will go again together at 7:06 AM.

4. We need to find the LCM of 10, 12 and 9 to know when they will step together again.
   LCM of (9, 10, 12) = 2 X 2 X 5 X 3 x 3 = 180.
   The kids will have to walk 180 steps, to cover the same distance.

5. The capacity of the container is the common divisor of 85 and 68.
   68 = 2 X 2 X 17 and 85 = 5 X 17. Thus, GCD is 17.
   So the maximum capacity of the container which can measure 85 and 68 l is 17 l.

Product Rule for HCF and LCM

6. Given numbers = 24 and 40

a. Product = 24 X 40 = 960

b. GCD of 24 and 40; GCD = 2 X 2 X 2 = 8

2	24	40
2	12	20
2	6	10
	3	5

LCM of 24 and 40;
LCM = 2 X2X2X5X3 = 120

2	24	40
2	12	20
2	6	10
5	3	5
3	3	1
	1	1

c. Product of GCD and LCM = 120 X 8 = 960 = Product of the given numbers.

d. Product of the GCD and LCM is the product of the given two numbers, which can be represented as GCD(24,40) x LCM(24,40) = 24 x 40.

Which Is the Best Buy?

7. Find the unit rate and compare.
   Offer 1:
   0.48 l = $24
   Cost of 1 l = 24/0.48 = $50
   Offer 2:
   2.4 l at the rate $ 96.12
   Cost of 1 l = 96.12/2.4 = $40.05
   Offer 3:
   2.7 l at the rate $ 94.50
   Cost of 1l = 94.50/ 2.7 = $35
   So the best buy will be Offer 3, 2.7 l at the rate of $94.50.

8. The smallest possible number is the LCM of 9 and 12

```
3 | 9    12
3 | 3    4
2 | 1    4
2 | 1    2
  | 1    1
```

LCM = 3 × 3 × 2 × 2 = 36.
Number on the door is 36.

9. Find the GCD of 15 and 18, so he can make as many equal pieces from the 2 sandwiches.

GCD of 18 and 15 is 3. So he can cut 3 inches from each.

```
3 | 18   15
  | 6    5
```

Total length of the sandwiches = 15+18 = 33 inches

Total number of individual servings = $\frac{33}{3}$ = 11. Thus, there will be 11 individual pieces.

10.

The Given points are

A (-4, 8) - II quadrant

B (5, 4) – I quadrant

C (-3, 0) – Negative X –axis

D (-7,-3) - III quadrant

E (7, 0) – Positive X-axis

F (5, -4) – IV Quadrant

11.

$0.5 = \frac{1}{2}$; $3.25 = 3\frac{1}{4} = \frac{13}{4}$; $1\frac{1}{2} = \frac{3}{2}$; $-2.1 = -2\frac{1}{10} = -\frac{21}{10}$

So the numbers are $\frac{1}{3}$; $\frac{1}{2}$; $\frac{2}{5}$; $\frac{13}{4}$; $\frac{3}{2}$; $-\frac{21}{10}$

LCM of the denominators (3, 2, 4, 5, 10) is 60

$\frac{1}{3} = \frac{20}{60}$; $\frac{1}{2} = \frac{30}{60}$; $\frac{2}{5} = \frac{24}{60}$; $\frac{13}{4} = \frac{195}{60}$

$\frac{3}{2} = \frac{90}{60}$; $-\frac{21}{10} = -\frac{126}{60}$, $\frac{195}{60}$

So the equivalent fractions are $\frac{20}{60}$; $\frac{30}{60}$; $\frac{24}{60}$; $\frac{90}{60}$; $-\frac{122}{60}$

Since the denominators are same greater the numerator, greater the value

So we can rearrange it as $-\frac{122}{60}$; $\frac{20}{60}$; $\frac{24}{60}$; $\frac{30}{60}$; $\frac{90}{60}$, $\frac{195}{60}$

Hence the given numbers can be re arranged from lowest to highest as

-2.1 ; $\frac{1}{3}$; $\frac{2}{5}$; 0.5 ; $1\frac{1}{2}$, 3.25

12.

a.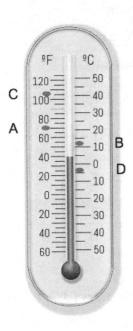

b. The thermometer reads 40°F and 4°C.

13.

a. Gain of $6 ; Gain is positive A = +6 = +6

b. Deposit of $10; Deposit is positive B = +10

c. Loss of 5; Loss is negative C = − 5

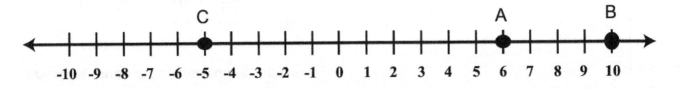

14.

a.

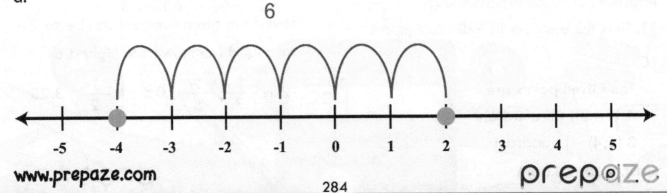

b.

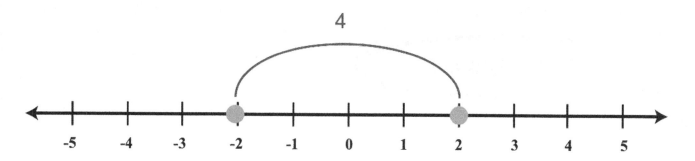

15.

A = 5 opposite of 5 = -5

B = 3 opposite of B = -3

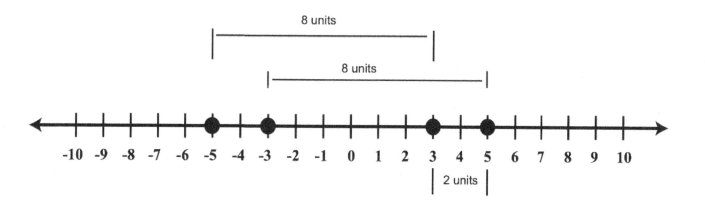

a. 5 is 2 units away from 3

b. -3 is 8 units away from 5 in the opposite direction

c. -5 to 3 is 8 units away in the opposite direction

Expressions and Equations

Solve the Inequalities

1.

a. e + 2 < 12

To obtain e on the left side subtract each term by 2.

e + 2 - 2 < 12 - 2

e < 10; e can be any value less than 10.

b. b - 4 ≥ 5

To obtain b on the left side add 4 to each term.

b - 4 + 4 ≥ 5 + 4

b ≥ 9; b can be any value equal to or greater than 9.

c. 2x > 2.4

To obtain x on the left side, divide each term by 2.

2x/2 > 2.4/2

x > 1.2; x can be any value greater than 1.2.

2.

a. r ≤ -3

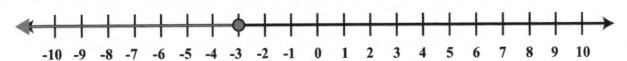

b. k ≥ 6

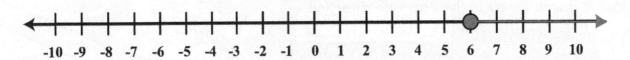

c. -5 > v

Determine the Solution

3. To determine x=8 is the solution to each of the following inequalities, we substitute the value of x in each of the inequalities.

a. 2x > 8

   Substituting the value of 8 in x, we get 16 > 8.
   Since it satisfies the inequality, it is a solution to the inequality.

b. x/4 ≤ 1

   Substituting the value of 8 in x, we get 2 ≤ 1.
   Since it does not satisfy the inequality it is not the solution.

c. 16 ≤ 4x + 4

   Substituting the value of 8 in x, we get 16 < 36.
   Since it satisfies the inequality, it is a solution to the inequality.

d. x + 1 < 10

   Substituting the value of 8 in x, we get 9 < 10.
   Since it satisfies the inequality, it is a solution to the inequality.

Hanger Problem

4. To identify the equations, add the variables on the left side of the hanger and the variables on the right side of the hanger and equate them.

a. Equation: s + 1 = 4
b. Equation: 3v = 3
c. Equation: 6 + k = 10

What Is the Inequality?

5.

a. x < 5

b. x > -1

c. x ≤ -2

Create Number Sentences

6. The answers may vary.

True or False?

7.

a. $3\frac{5}{6} = 1\frac{2}{3} \times 2\frac{1}{6}$;

$\frac{23}{6} \neq \frac{65}{18}$

Thus it is false.

b. $\frac{12}{4} \leq 3$;

$3 \leq 3$

Thus it is true.

c. $121 - 98 \geq 23$;

$23 \geq 23$

Thus it is true.

d. $\frac{54}{10} = 5.4$;

Thus it is false.

Can Richard Play in the Ball Pit?

8.

a. Any value less than 36 can be written.

b. Let us assume the height of the kid to be 'h', thus, h < 36.

c. Any value greater than 36 can be written.

d. No, she cannot play in the pit because her height is greater than 36.

e. Number line depicting the inequality h < 36

9.

Equation	Action	Equivalent equation
X = 6	Add 2 to both sides of the equation.	X + 2 = 8
X = 10	Multiply 5 to both sides of the equation.	5 × X = 10 × 5 5X = 50
X = 24	Divide both sides of the equation by 4.	$\frac{X}{6} = \frac{24}{4}$ $\frac{X}{4} = 6$
X = 9	Multiply both sides of the equation 6.	6 × X = 9 × 6 6X = 54
5 = x	Subtract both sides of the equation by 5.	5 - 5 = X - 5 0 = X - 5

Word Problems

10.

a. $C = \frac{5}{9}(F-32)$

$C = \frac{5}{9} \times (78-32)$

$C = \frac{5}{9} \times (46)$

Thus, 25.556 °C

b. Cost per ticket = $6

Total money spent = $198

Number of students who went on the field trip = $\frac{\$198}{\$6}$

Therefore, number of students = 33

c. Cards per page = 5

Total number of cards Ricky has = 45

Total number of pages to buy = $\frac{45}{5}$

Therefore, total number of pages = 9

d. T-shirt cost = $20

Shipping Charges (per tee) = $10

Total cost (per tee) = $30

Total money earned = $1380

Number of shirts ordered = $\frac{1380}{30}$

Therefore, shirts ordered = 46

www.prepaze.com

11.

a.

Expression: x + 2

i.

x	x + 2
0	0+2 = 2
1	1+2 = 3
3	3+2 = 5
6	6+2 = 8

ii.
1. To obtain the value of x, equate x+2 to 5
2. Subtract 2 from both the sides
x+2 = 5
x+2-2=5-2
Thus, x=3

iii.
1. To obtain the value of x, equate x+2 to 7
2. Subtract 2 from both the sides
x+2=7
x+2-2=7-2
Thus, x=5

b.

Expression: 5y

i.

y	5y
1	5 × 1 = 5
4	5 × 4 = 20
5	5 × 5 = 25
10	5 × 10 = 50

ii. To obtain the value of y equate 5y to 10.

5y = 10

Thus, y = 2

iii. To obtain the value of y equate 5y to 20.

5y = 20

Thus, y = 4

12.

a. **Equation:** x + 4 = 1

Pan balance:

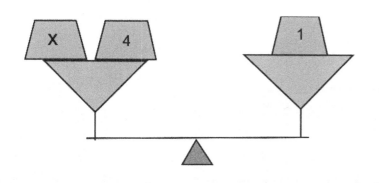

Fact families:

1 − 4 = x

1 − x = 4

Isolating the variable:

x = 1 − 4

x = −3

b. **Equation:** 2x=6

   Pan balance:

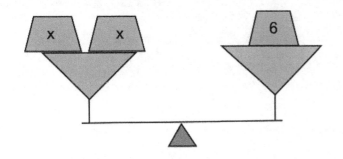

Fact families:

$x = \dfrac{6}{2}$

$2 = \dfrac{6}{2x}$

Isolating the variable:

$x = \dfrac{6}{2}$

$x = 3$

---

c. **Equation:** 7x = 7

   Pan balance:

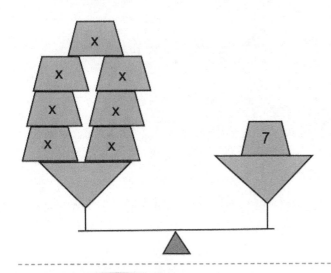

Fact families:

$x = \dfrac{7}{7}$

$7 = \dfrac{7}{x}$

Isolating the variable:

$x = \dfrac{7}{7}$

$x = 1$

Riddle Time

Show your working here:

1. Assume the number to be x
   Divide the number by 5
   Equate it to 8
   Solve the equation
   $\dfrac{x}{5} = 8$
   Thus x=40

2. Assume the number to be x
   Multiply the number by 4
   Equate it to 24
   Solve the equation
   4x=24
   Thus x=6

14.

a.

Story problem:

Nina read 9 more books than Ben in the first marking period. Write an expression for the number of books Nina read.

Description with units:

Let n represent the number of books Ben read

Expression:

Number of books Nina read: n + 9

Evaluate the Expression If:

Ben read 8 books in the first marking period.

Show Your Work and Evaluate:

n = 8
n + 9 = 8 + 9 = 17

Thus, Nina read 17 books

b.

Story problem:

Felix scored 6 fewer goals than Ivan in the first half of the season. Write an expression for the number of goals Felix scored.

Description with units:

Let I represent Ivans goals, F represent Felix's goals

Expression:

$I - 6 = F$

Evaluate the Expression If:

Ivan scored 16 goals.

Show Your Work and Evaluate:

$F = I - 6$

$F = 16 - 6 = 10$

Thus, Felix scored 10 goals.

Angles at the Parking Lot

15.

a. The angle x is 65° because 115° and angle x are supplementary angles. Both the angles add up to 180°, thus 180° - 115° = 65°.
Similarly, angle y is 65° because 115° and angle y are supplementary angles. Both the angles add up to 180°, thus 180° - 115° = 65°.

b. $115° + x° = 180°$
115° and angle x are supplementary angles. The two angles have a sum of 180°.

c. $115° + x° = 180°$
$x° = 180° - 115° = 65°$.

d. $115° + y° = 180°$
115° and angle y are supplementary angles. The two angles have a sum of 180°.

16.

a. $x° + 66° = 90°$
$x° = 90° - 66°$
$x° = 24°$

b. The two angles have a sum of 90°.

c. $x° + 66° = 90°$

17.

a.

∠ABD 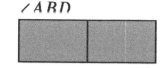   ∠DBC

b. 3 units or 3x = 90°
1 unit or x = 30°
2 units or 2x = 60°
∠ABD is 60°.
∠DBC is 30°.

c. $2x° + x° = 90°$

d. $2x° + x° = 90°$
$3x° = 90°$
$3x° \div 3 = 90° \div 3$
$x° = 30°$
$2x° = 2(30°) = 60°$

18.

$x° + 44° + 33° = 180°$
$x° + 77° = 180°$
$x° = 180° - 77°$
$x° = 103°$

Determine the Tiles to Fit the Corner

19. $x° + 42° = 90°$

$x° + 42° - 42° = 90° - 42°$

$x° = 48°$

Posters and Fliers

20.

a.

Independent Variable: Number of weeks worked

Dependent Variable: Number of poster or fliers designed

b.

Number of Weeks	Number of poster or fliers designed
1	3
2	6
3	9
4	12
5	15

c.

The equation is $d = 3w$, where w is the number of weeks worked and d is the number of posters and fliers designed.

21.

a. Total cost per day, in dollars $c = 2.25m + 8$

Where, **c** is the total cost, **m** is the additional hour

b. Independent variable = Number of hours
Dependent Variable = Total cost in dollars.

c.

Number of hours	Total cost in dollars (c)
4	2.25 × 1 + 8 = 10.25
5	2.25 × 2 + 8 = 12.5
6	2.25 × 3 + 8 = 14.75
7	2.25 × 4 + 8 = 17
8	2.25 × 5 + 8 = 19.25
9	2.25 × 6 + 8 = 21.5
10	2.25 × 7 + 8 = 23.75

Noah's Saving Plan

22. Each week Noah earns $20.

a.

Week	Amount saved
1	20
2	40
3	60
4	80
5	100
6	120
7	140
8	160
9	180
10	200

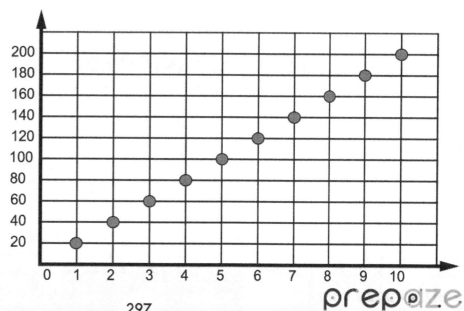

b. $s = 20w$

Independent Variable = Number of weeks

Dependent Variable = Amount of money saved

23.

a. $d + 7 = 21$

To obtain the value of the variable, we subtract 7 from both the sides.

$d + 7 - 7 = 21 - 7$

Thus, $d = 14$

b. $e + 8 \geq 31$

To obtain the value of the variable, we subtract 8 from both the sides.

$e + 8 - 8 \geq 31 - 8$

Thus, $e = 23$

c. $2f = 30$

To obtain the value of the variable, we divide it by 2 on both the sides.

$$\frac{2f}{2} = \frac{30}{2}$$

Thus, $f = 15$

24.

a. Assume the variable to be s.

Thus, $s \leq 2$

b. Assume the variable to be r.

Thus, $r \geq 30$

c. Money she earns per hour = $20/hour

Money she needs to go to the concert = $100 (atleast)

Number of hours she needs to work (h) $= \frac{100}{20} = 5$ (atleast)

Thus, $h \geq 5$

Complete the Table

25.

Exponent Form	Series of Product	Standard Form
2^3	2 x 2 x 2	8
3^4	3 X 3 X 3 X 3	81
1.1^2	1.1 X 1.1	1.21
$\left(\frac{1}{2}\right)^6$	$\frac{1}{2} \times \frac{1}{2} \times \frac{1}{2} \times \frac{1}{2} \times \frac{1}{2} \times \frac{1}{2}$	$\frac{1}{64}$

26. 2x + 3y can be pictorially represented as

| 2x | 3y |

Therefore 3(2x + 3y) =

| 2x | 3y | 2x | 3y | 2x | 3y |
3(2x+3y)

Rearranging the 2x and 3y we have

| 6x | | | 9y | | |
| 2x | 2x | 2x | 3y | 3y | 3y |

Therefore 3(2x + 3y) = 6x + 9y.

Area and Perimeter

27. Perimeter is the sum of all sides of the given figure = x + 2x + x + x + x + 2x + x + x = 10x

Area is the product of its length and breadth = x (x + 2x + x) = x (4x) = $4x^2$.

28. a. $4^2 - 3^3$ = 4 x 4 − 3 x 3 x 3
= 16 − 27 = -11

b. $2(\frac{1}{2})(3(1) - (-1)) = 3 + 1 = 4$

29. a. Volume of the box = length x breadth x height

Let l = length ; b = breadth ; h = height for the given cuboid

Breath = 2 times the length l, therefore b = 2l

Height = 3 times the length l, therefore h = 3l

Volume = l x b x h = l X 2l X 3l = $6l^3$

b. When l = 4 cm

Volume = 6 x 4^3 = 6 x 4 x 4 x 4 = 384 cm^3

When b = 4 cm

length: breadth: height = 1: 2: 3

when breadth = 4

length = $\frac{1}{2}$ (4) = 2

Height = 2 X 3 = 6

Volume = 4 x 2 x 6 = 48 cm^3

Is Ron Right?

30. No.

25 − (4 X 3 + 5) = 25 − (12 + 5) = 25 − 17 = 8

Geometry

1. Area= base x perpendicular height
   Base = 40 ft
   Height = 20 ft
   Area = 40 x 20
   Therefore, area = 800 sqft

2. Area = base x height
   Base = 10ft
   Height = 25ft
   Area = 10 x 25
   Therefore, area = 250 sqft

3.
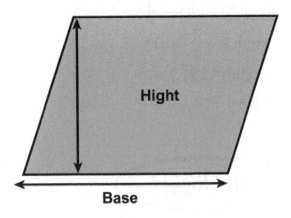

4.
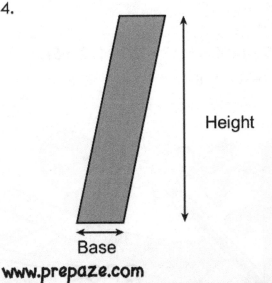

5. To find the area of the parallelogram we must use the following formula:
   Area = base x perpendicular height
   Base = 24 ft
   Height = 12 ft
   Area = 24 x 12
   Therefore, area = 288 sqft
   To find the area of the rectangle we must use the following formula:
   Area = length x breadth
   Length = 24ft
   Breadth =12ft
   Area = 24 x 12
   Therefore, area=288 sqft
   The area of the rectangle and parallelogram are the same.

Drek's Swimming Pool

6.
   a. To find the number of tiles we need to find the area of triangle using the following formula:
      Area = $\frac{1}{2}$ x base x height
      Base = 400yd
      Height = 75yd
      Area = $\frac{1}{2}$ x 400 x 75
      Therefore, area = 15,000 sq yd
      Thus he needs 15,000 tiles altogether.

b. Find the area of the triangle and rectangle and add them.

Area of the triangle = $\frac{1}{2}$ x base x height

Base = 400yd

Height = 75yd

Area = $\frac{1}{2}$ x 400 x 75

Area = 15,000 sq yd

Area = length x breadth

Length = 100yd

Breadth = 75yd

Area = 100 x 75

Area = 7,500 sq yd

Total area = 15,000 + 7,500 = 22,500 sq yd

Therefore, the total area of the pool is 22,500 sq yd.

a.

Lucy's Kitchen Counter

Counter A	Counter B
Area of counter A = Area of rectangle + Area of square.	Area of counter B = Area of rectangle + Area of square.
Area of rectangle = length x breadth	Area of rectangle = length x breadth
For length: (15,16)(5,16)	For Length: (16,2)(5,2)
Length = 15 - 5 = 10	Length = 16 - 5 = 11
For Breadth: (5,19)(5,16)	For Breadth: (16,5)(16,2)
Breadth = 19 - 16 = 3	Breadth = 5 - 2 = 3
Area = 10 x 3 = 30 sq ft	Area = 11 x 3 = 33 sq ft
Area of square = side x side	Area of square = side x side
Points taken (8,12)(8,16)	Points taken (5,8)(5,5)
Side = 16-12 = 4	Side = 8 - 5 = 3
Area = 4 x 4 = 16 sq ft	Area = 3 x 3 = 9 sq ft
Total Area = 30 + 16 = 46 sq ft	Total Area = 33 + 9 = 42 sq ft

Since the counter A has a greater area, Lucy should choose it.

www.prepaze.com

b.

Counter A	Counter B
Perimeter of A = Perimeter of rectangle + Perimeter of square - 2(overlapping sides) Perimeter of rectangle = 2(l + b) = 2(10 + 3) = 26 ft Perimeter of square = 4 × side = 4 × 4 = 16 ft Overlapping side length = 4 ft Total perimeter = 26 + 16 - 2(4) = 42 - 8 = 34 ft	Perimeter of B = Perimeter of rectangle + perimeter of square - 2(overlapping sides) Perimeter of rectangle = 2(l + b) = 2(11 + 3) = 28 ft Perimeter of square = 4 × side = 4 × 3 = 12 ft overlapping side length = 3 ft Total perimeter = 28 + 12 - 2(3) = 40 - 6 = 34 ft

Since, both the counters have the same perimeter, she can choose any one of the counters.

8. Area = $\frac{1}{2}$ × base × height = $\frac{1}{2}$ × 14 × 12 = 84 sq inch

Area of a School

9.

a. Area of each part of the school:

Area of the green and red triangle :
Area: $\frac{1}{2}$ × 44 × 10
Area: 220 sq km

Area of the pink and blue triangle:
Area: $\frac{1}{2}$ × 44 × 10
Area: 220 sq km

Area of the rectangle:
Area: 40 × 44 = 1760 sq km

b. Area of the whole school:
220 sq km + 220 sq km + 1760 sq km
= 2,200 sqkm

10.

a. To find the volume of the prism, we use the formula: length x breadth x height

Length: $3\frac{1}{2}$ = 3.50 cm

Breadth: $2\frac{1}{2}$ = 2.50 cm

Height: 4 cm

Therefore, volume = 35 cubic cm

b. Arrangement of cubes is as follows:

along length: $3\frac{1}{2} \div \frac{1}{2}$ = 7 cubes

along breadth: $2\frac{1}{2} \div \frac{1}{2}$ = 5 cubes

along height: $4 \div \dfrac{1}{2} = 8$ cubes

Total number of cubes required to fill
$= 7 \times 5 \times 8 = 280$ cubes

c. Volume of each small cube $= \dfrac{1}{2} \times \dfrac{1}{2} \times \dfrac{1}{2} = 1/8$ cubic cm

Total number of cubes required = 280

volume × total number of cubes $= \dfrac{1}{8} \times 280 = 35$ cubic cm = volume of the prism.

d. Why is the number of cubes needed different than the volume?

Because the cubes are not 1 cm each, the volume is different from the number of cubes. However, I could multiply the number of cubes by the volume of one cube and still get the original volume.

11.

a. Volume of cube

Volume = side × side × side

Side $= 6\dfrac{1}{2} = \dfrac{13}{2} = 6.5$ in.

Therefore, volume = 6.5 × 6.5 × 6.5 = 274.625 cubic in.

Volume = 274.625 cubic in.

Volume of the gift box

length × breadth × height

Length: 16 in.

Breadth: 13 in.

Height: $\dfrac{13}{2} = 6.5$ in.

Therefore, volume $= 16 \times \dfrac{13}{2} \times 13 = 1352$ cubic in.

Volume = 1352 cubic in.

b. Arrangement of cube-shaped boxes in the rectangular box is as follows:

along length: $16 \div 6\dfrac{1}{2} = 2$ cubes (approx..)

along breadth: $13 \div 6\dfrac{1}{2} = 2$ cubes

along height: $6\dfrac{1}{2} \div 6\dfrac{1}{2} = 1$ cube

Total number of cube-shaped boxes that can be packed in the gift box = 2 × 2 × 1 = 4 boxes

An Aquarium Math Problem

12.

a. Volume = length × width × height ; v = l × h × w cubic meters.

64.224 = 6.4 × 4.2 × w

b. To find the width we must rearrange the above formula, that is

Width = Volume/(length × height)

Length: 6.4 m

Height: 4.2m

Volume: 64.224

Width $= \dfrac{64.224}{(6.4 \times 4.2)} = 2.4$ m (rounded off to the nearest ten)

Therefore, the width is 2.4 m

13.

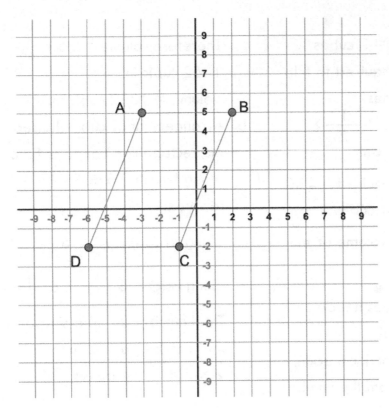

Height = 5 - (-2) = 7

Base = -1 - (-6) = -1 + 6 = 5

Area of the parallelogram = base x height = 7 x 5 = 35 sq. units.

14. To find the other two coordinates, we must find the length of the rectangle with area 72.

Points are (5,-8)(5,4)

In order to find the length we need to subtract the second coordinate from the first. That is:

Length = X-axis = 5 - 5 = 0

Breadth = Y-axis = 4 - (-8) = 12

Since the breadth is 12, the length is found out by rearranging the formula

Area = length x breadth

Length = $\dfrac{Area}{breadth} = \dfrac{72}{12} = 6$

Inorder to find the coordinates we must subtract 6 from the given x coordinates and retain the y coordinates.

Therefore, 5 - 6 = -1

Therefore the 3rd coordinate is (-1, -8)

Therefore the 4th coordinate is (-1, 4)

Football Ground Math Problem

15.

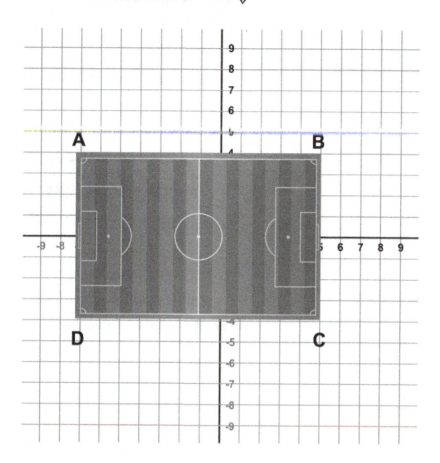

a.

Points	Coordinates
A	-7,4
B	5,4
C	5,-4
D	-7,-4

b. Size of each grid = 10m

To find the length of each side we must use the coordinates

To find the length, we use the coordinates D,C

D - (-7,-4)

C - (5,-4)

We subtract D from C:

X-coordinates = 5 - (-7) = 12

Y-coordinates = -4-(-4) = 0

To cross check We can count the number of squares from the coordinate D to the coordinate C

Therefore, the number of squares from D to C are 12 squares.

Length = 12 x 10m = 120m

To find the breadth, we use the coordinates A,D

A - (-7,4)

D - (-7,-4)

We subtract D from A:

X-coordinates = -7-(-7) = 0

Y-coordinates = 4-(-4) = 8

To cross check We can count the number of squares from the coordinate D to the coordinate A.

Therefore, the number of squares from D to A are 8 squares.

Length = 8 x 10m = 80m

c. To find the area of the ground, we use the formula:

Area = length x breadth

Length = 120m

Breadth = 80m

Area = 120 x 80 = 9600 sq m

Therefore, the area of the ground is 9600 sq m.

A Juicy Problem

16. Any net corresponding to a rectangular prism and a triangular prism. A sample is given.

a.

12 inches high

3 inches wide

6 inches long

b.

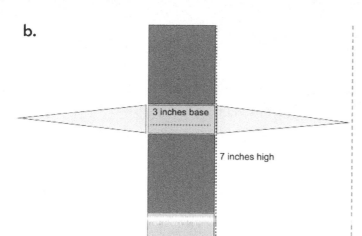

17. Name: Square Based Pyramid

Surface area: To find the surface area of this shape, we need to find the area of all the 5 shapes: four triangles and the rectangular base. Then we need to add all the areas.

Area of rectangle:
Area= length x breadth
length= 4ft
breadth=3ft
Area= 4x3
Therefore, area=12sqft

Area of triangle(length as the base):
Area= $\frac{1}{2}$ xbasexheight
base= 4ft
height=3ft
Area= $\frac{1}{2}$ x 4 x 3
Therefore, area=6sqft

Area of triangle(breadth as the base):
Area= $\frac{1}{2}$ xbasexperpendicular height
base=3ft
height=3ft
Area= $\frac{1}{2}$ x 3 x 3
Therefore, area=4.5sqft

Total Surface Area
Therefore, the total surface area is Area of triangle1(length as the base)+Area of triangle2(length as the base)+Area of triangle3(breadth as the base)+Area of triangle4(breadth as the base)+Area of the rectangle.
Area= 6+6+4.5+4.5+12=33
Therefore the total surface area is 33 sq ft.

Help Jessica Make Gift Boxes

18.

a. List all the possible whole number dimensions for the box.

Since cube root of 20 is 2.7, it is not possible for her to make a box out of a cube.

For a cuboid, the factors of 20 have to be found.

Factors: 1,2,4,5,10,20

Therefore the possible whole number dimensions are:
1x1x20
1x2x10
1x4x5
2x2x5

b. Which possibility requires the least amount of material to make?

To find out the least amount of material taken, we must find the surface area using all the dimensions.

Surface area formula = 2((length x breadth) + (breadth x height) + (height x length))

1. Dimension 1: 1x1x20
Length=1cm
Breadth=1cm
Height=20cm
S.A = 2((1x1)+(1x20)+(1x20)) = 2x41 = 82
S.A = 82 cubic cm

2. Dimension 2: 1x2x10
Length=1cm
Breadth=2 cm
Height=10cm
S.A = 2((1x2)+(10x2)+(1x10)) = 2x32 = 64
S.A = 64 cubic cm

3. Dimension 3: 1x4x5
Length=1cm
Breadth=4cm
Height=5cm
S.A = 2((1x4)+(4x5)+(5x1)) = 2x29 = 58
S.A = 58 cubic cm

4. Dimension 4: 2x2x5
Length=2cm
Breadth=2cm
Height=5cm
S.A = 2((2x2)+(2x5)+(5x2)) = 2x24
S.A = 48 cubic cm

The box with dimensions 2 × 2 × 5 requires least amount of material to make.

c. Which box would you recommend her to use? Why?

Since the box with dimensions 2x2x5 uses the least material with the surface area 48 cubic cm, it is the best option to use.

Statistics and Probability

Categorical or Numerical Data Sets

1.
a. Numerical - N

Since the height of 10 pet dogs can be easily measured it is considered to be numerical.

b. Categorical - C

Since the number of dance forms performed by 20 adults cannot be added it is a categorical variable.

c. Categorical - C

Since the favorite fruit of each person in a group of 20 adults cannot be added it is a categorical variable.

d. Categorical - C

Since the number of pets for each of 30 sixth graders cannot be added it is a categorical value.

Lunch Hour at Big Burgers

2. To calculate the mean we use the formula= sum of the terms/number of terms

a. Mean

Sum of the number of burgers sold= 350 + 300 + 325 + 340 + 400 + 250 + 450=2415

Number of days=7

Therefore, Mean=$\frac{2415}{7}$=345

Mean number of burgers sold in a week=345

b. Absolute Mean Deviation
- Find the mean of all values
- Find the distance of each value from that mean (subtract the mean from each value, ignore minus signs)
- Then find the mean of those distances
- Ignore the minus sign

Day of the week	Mean Deviation Number of burgers sold - Mean (345)
Monday	350 - 345 = 5
Tuesday	300 - 345 = 45
Wednesday	325 - 345 = 20
Thursday	340 - 345 = 5
Friday	400 - 345 = 55
Saturday	250 - 345 = 95
Sunday	450 - 345 = 105

Sum of the mean deviation terms= 5+45+20+5+55+95+105 = 330

Number of days=7

Therefore, mean deviation = $\frac{330}{7}$ = 47.142

Therefore, the absolute mean deviation of burgers sold in a week is 47.142.

c.

Burger type	Calories rounded off to the nearest 100
Cheeseburger - 1	300
Double cheeseburger - 2	400
Triple cheeseburger - 3	800
Chilli burger - 4	400
Soy burger - 5	100
Veggie burger - 6	100
Turkey burger - 7	200
Ground beef burger - 8	200

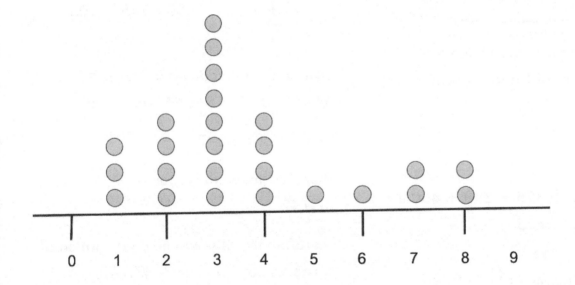

Types of burgers

● - One dot represents 100 calories

d. The calories mostly range from 100 - 400 .

Kyle's Christmas Tree

a.

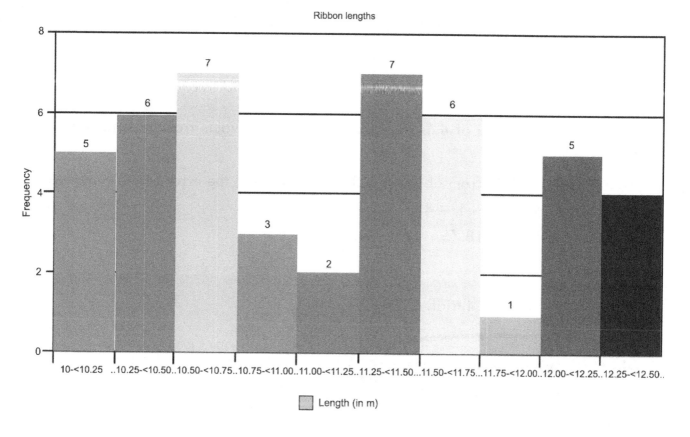

b. The histogram is not symmetric.

c. Answers may vary. There are more observations greater than 11 metres.

d. MAD > 0.25

A Science Experiment

4.

a.

- To calculate the mean we use the formula = sum of the terms/Number Of terms

- Since mean and number of trials are given, we need to rearrange the formula to find the total time for the trials.
- Therefore total time for trials = mean x number of trials

Number of trials = 5

Mean = 3.75

Total time for trials = 3.75 x 5 = 18.75

Therefore, the total time for trials is 18.75 minutes

b.

- Since there is an error of 4.6s we need to subtract the value from the total time for the trials.
- We divide the value from above by ONLY 4 trials, since the error trial is removed.
- Number of trials = 5 - 1 = 4

Total time for trials = 18.75 - 4.6 = 14.15

Mean = $\dfrac{14.15}{4}$ = 3.5

Therefore, the mean of 4 trials is 3.5

5.

a. There are 20 observations.

b. Answers may vary.

Shape : Not symmetric

Center: there are 2 peaks

Variability: When the median is selected as the measure of center for a typical value (because the distribution is not approximately symmetric), then the interquartile range would be selected as the measure of variability.

c.

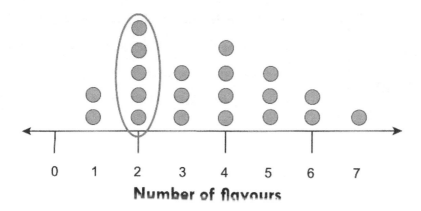

The best response is 2.

A. I expect the mean to be larger than the median. Since there are more ice creams in the 2nd flavour and the graph is left skewed, the mean is greater than the median.

d. Since inter quartile range can be used to tell when some of the other values are too far from the central value, it is a better choice.

e.
- Mean: Increases by 1
- Median: Remains the same
- Mean Absolute Deviation: Increases by approximately 3.6
- Interquartile Range: Increases by 4

6. Answers will vary. 80 would be the test score that all 31 students would have if all 31 students had the same score.

7.

a.

Time - Koolz	Frequency	Time - Karlz	Frequency
0	-	0	-
5	2	5	1
10	6	10	4
15	4	15	3
20	8	20	5
25	7	25	7
30	4	30	3

1. Kools Box Plot Summary

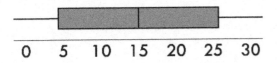

Kools five - number summary:
5,10,15,20,25,30

2. Karlz Box Plot Summary

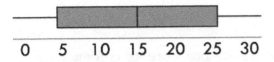

Karlz five - number summary:
5,10,15,20,25,30

b. The dot plot shows individual times, which you cannot see in the box plot. The box plot shows the location of the median and of the lower and upper quartiles

How Many Pets Does Noah's Friends Have?

b. If the friend having 4 pets shares his pet with a friend having only 2 pets, we need to add 1 pet to the 4th column and subtract 1 pet from the 2nd column.

c.

d.

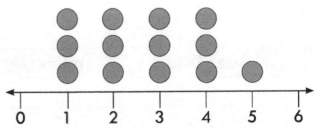

Number of pets each had

8.

a.

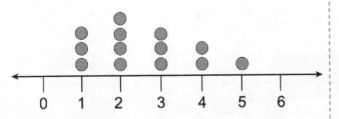

Number of pets each had

9.

a.

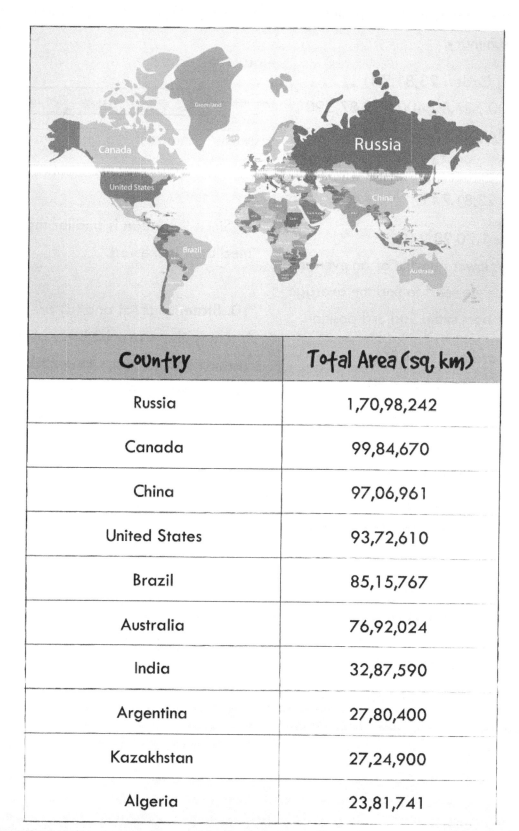

Country	Total Area (sq. km)
Russia	1,70,98,242
Canada	99,84,670
China	97,06,961
United States	93,72,610
Brazil	85,15,767
Australia	76,92,024
India	32,87,590
Argentina	27,80,400
Kazakhstan	27,24,900
Algeria	23,81,741

- We need to arrange all the numbers in ascending order to find the five-number summary.

- Ascending Order: 23,81,741 , 27,24,900 , 27,80,400 , 32,87,590 , 76,92,024 , 85,15,767 , 93,72,610 , 97,06,961 , 99,84,670 , 1,70,98,242

- Minimum: 23,81,741

- Maximum: 1,70,98,242
  To find the lower quartile of an even set of numbers we need to find the average of the numbers in the 2nd,3rd position.

- Lower Quartile: (27,24,900 + 27,80,400)/2= 27,52,650

- Median: (76,92,024 + 85,15,767)/2 = 81,03,895.5
  To find the upper quartile of an even set of numbers we need to find the average of the numbers in the 8th and 9th position.

- Upper quartile: (97,06,961 + 99,84,670)/2=98,45,815. 5

b.

- Interquartile Range is found by subtracting the lower quartile from the upper quartile.
  Upper Quartile: 98,45,815.5
  Lower Quartile: 27,52,650

Inter Quartile: 98,45,815.5 - 27,52,650 = 70.93,165.5

c.

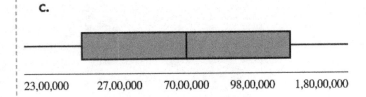

d. Since the mean is smaller than the median it is skewed.

10. Statements (a) and (b) are true because there are 10 bags above 82 kernels and 10 bags below 82 kernels. Also, statement (e) is true because that happened once, so it could probably happen again.

Science Answer Key
Earth Sciences - Plate Tectonics and Earth's Structure

Across:
2. midoceanridges
3. pangea
4. trench
7. continentaldrift

Down:
1. asthenosphere
3. platetectonics
4. tre (trench down)
5. subduction
6. oceanicplate

Causes and Effects of Plate Boundaries

Name of the plate boundaries	What causes it?	What are the effects?
Transform fault boundary	A lithospheric plate boundary where two plates slide by each other.	Movement of transform fault boundaries causes earthquakes.

Name of the plate boundaries	What causes it?	What are the effects?
Divergent boundary	A lithospheric plate boundary where two plates move apart.	The convection cell causes the plates to move apart. As they move apart, molten rock occupies the space between and solidies. This is the process by which new Earth's surface is created.

Name of the plate boundaries	What causes it?	What are the effects?
Convergent boundary	A lithospheric plate boundary where two plates come together.	When two plates collide under water, where one is an oceanic plate and the other is a continental plate or when both the plates are oceanic, the oceanic plate subducts the continental plate. This forms a trench. When two continental plates collide, they are too buoyant to be subducted. Over time they form mountains.

Tectonic Plates Around the World

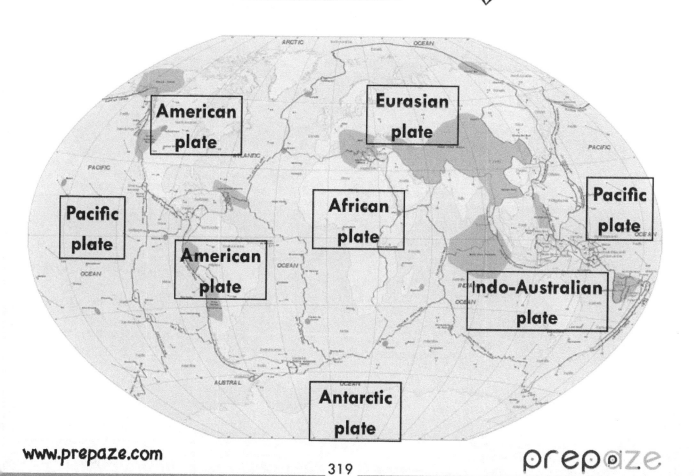

Research on Natural Disasters

1
a. When lithospheric plates slide past each other, there is friction. This, over time, causes the Earth's crust above the plates to move. This sudden movement is called an earthquake.

b. Tsunami is caused when an earthquake occurs under water, on the ocean floor. Waves are much taller during a tsunami.

2. Focus - point below the surface of the Earth where the rocks break.

Fault - a region on the Earth's surface that is split into two pieces

Epicenter - point on the Earth's surface above the focus where the earthquake is the strongest

3.
a. Palu-Koro fault

b. 7 meters / 29 feet

c. 7.5

d. Donggala regency, Central Sulawesi, Indonesia

Layers of the Earth

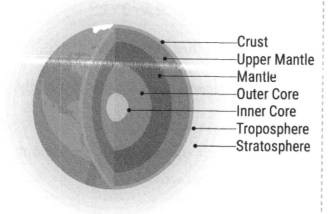

1. Inner core - mostly made of iron. It is solid and hot due to enormous pressure and temperature.
   Outer core - made of iron which is in molten state. It is liquid. It creates Earth's magnetic field.
   Lower mantle - It is placed just above the core. It is made of rock and it is warm. It includes the aesthenosphere.
   Upper mantle - Comprises of the lithosphere. It is thin.
   Lithosphere - It comprises of the tectonic plates that move the Earth's surface
   Aesthenosphere - Lies just below the lithosphere and forms the outermost part of the lower mantle. It is slushy region with hot rock and molten rock.

2.
   A. True.
   B. False. The temperature of the inner core is about 7200°C.
   C. True.
   D. False. The distance to the center of the Earth is about 5100 km.
   E. False. The aesthenosphere is a part of the lower mantle.

Faults and Earthquakes

1. Zig-zags creeks, breaks formed by the movement of transform faults
   Earthquakes - areas where there are earthquakes often, will have transform faults

2. The San Andreas fault. It lies between the Pacific plate and the North American Plate.

Analyze an Earthquake

Body Waves	Surface Waves
• Seismic waves that travel through the Earth's interior. • There are two main kinds of waves - P (primary) waves and S (secondary waves). • P waves are faster that push and pull through the rocks. • They have a side to side motion, perpendicular to the direction of movement.	• Body waves that reach the surface. • They are slower than the slowest body waves. • They have an up and down movement, like the ocean waves. • They cause the maximum damage to property.

2. Seismographs detect the P waves first as they are the fastest, followed by S waves as they are slower than P waves as the liquid core acts as a barrier to its movement. The last waves that get recorded are the surface waves as they are the slowest waves.

3.

Station Name	S-P wave time difference (in seconds) - x axis	Distance to epicenter (in km) - y axis
A	30	110
B	35	130
C	40	150

a.
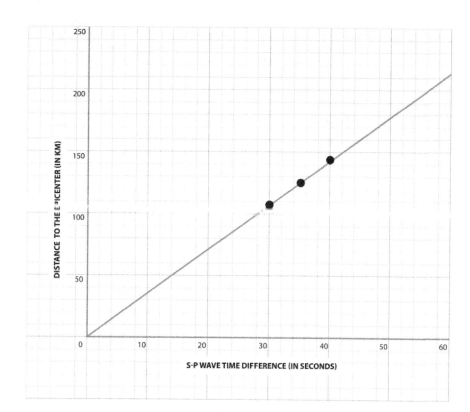

b.
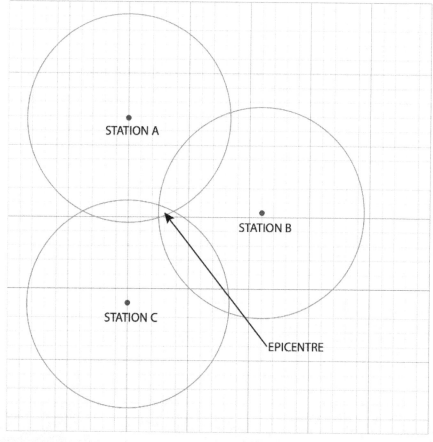

Earth Sciences - Shaping Earth's Surface

Factors that Shape the Earth

Shaping the Surface of the Earth

1. The process of breaking rock is called <u>weathering</u>.

2. <u>Frost wedging</u> is a process where frozen water inside cracks present in rocks cause it to break down.

3. Frozen water which grinds the valley floor with pieces of rocks lodged in it are called <u>glaciers</u>.

4. Old statue surfaces have been worn away due reactions between water and the rock surface in the process of <u>chemical weathering</u>.

5. Plants growing roots into small crevices and exert force on the rock. This breaks down the rocks into smaller pieces. This process is called <u>root wedging</u>.

6. Small pieces and grains of weathered rocks formed by flowing rivers are called <u>sediments</u>.

7. Grains settling in order, based on their size due to the flow of water is called <u>graded bedding</u>.

8. A stream that has many channels that criss-cross each other is called a <u>braided stream</u>.

9. S-shaped curves formed by rivers are called <u>meanders</u>.

H	H	N	F	M	R	G	R	E	D	E	D	S	A	W	E	N	I	N	G
B	R	I	R	N	G	W	T	E	R	I	S	A	U	Y	U	P	G	P	O
B	N	M	O	J	X	L	N	E	F	G	H	J	Z	C	O	N	S	S	D
H	I	L	S	K	T	V	Y	N	H	G	R	D	B	M	I	N	E	J	X
W	E	A	T	H	E	R	I	N	G	V	E	T	N	R	E	Y	D	K	A
A	I	M	W	E	D	A	T	N	O	O	N	E	E	M	E	A	I	L	O
U	B	N	E	B	D	J	E	K	F	G	K	H	S	A	L	D	M	S	P
D	B	N	D	W	Q	O	P	M	L	N	T	J	V	E	Y	N	E	R	L
B	R	I	G	D	N	J	I	K	M	A	L	S	N	R	S	N	N	E	L
H	K	N	I	B	B	T	R	I	E	H	A	L	P	T	A	I	T	I	X
O	V	M	N	I	A	Q	L	W	H	K	U	N	V	S	I	K	S	C	D
B	L	B	G	J	I	D	L	C	R	O	S	S	C	D	U	R	T	A	L
R	A	M	N	A	G	A	R	V	A	D	A	V	A	E	E	L	L	L	I
D	E	M	O	N	C	T	Y	R	O	O	T	W	E	D	G	I	N	G	K
N	A	L	V	I	A	R	N	A	G	A	R	I	N	I	L	O	O	K	I
M	E	R	M	S	A	L	K	I	T	H	A	A	B	A	B	A	I	L	I
N	A	E	G	N	I	D	D	E	B	D	E	D	A	R	G	S	A	R	K
G	H	U	M	M	U	N	U	P	O	M	D	A	V	B	E	N	N	A	I
C	O	C	A	R	O	K	O	N	U	K	O	H	B	I	T	Y	L	A	Q

Journey through the Meander

The answers must include the following terms:

S shaped curve, water speed - slowest on the inside and fastest on the outside

Point bar / deposits on the inside of the bank

Types of Rocks

1. False. Clay and silt are the finest particles which together form mudstone.

2. False. A conglomerate is formed from pebbles and silt.

3. True.

4. False. The order in which sedimentary rock layers are formed from larger to smaller is called direction of younging.

5. False. In a graded bedding pattern, the finest particles are on top.

6. False. When sediment settles on the bottom of the lake, the larger pieces settle first, at the bottom.

7. False. Young mountains have sharp peaks with no vegetation while old mountains have rounded tops with vegetation.

8. True.

9. False. Longshore drift occurs when waves move toward the shore at an angle and leave in a different direction.

10. False. Beaches can lose a lot of sand at submarine canyon locations.

1. flooding
2. wildfire
3. flashflood
4. richterscale
5. slumping
6. liguefaction
7. shield
8. tsunami
9. volcanicash
10. hurricane
11. volcaniceruption

Earth Sciences - Energy in the Earth System

Sun – Major Source of Energy for Weather

Journey in a Lahar

The answer must include the following points:

Lahars are mudflows resulting from water mixing with loose soil on the steep side of volcanos.

They often carry huge rocks and boulders.

They follow the river path and bring the rocks and boulders into town.

Ocean Currents

1 & 2

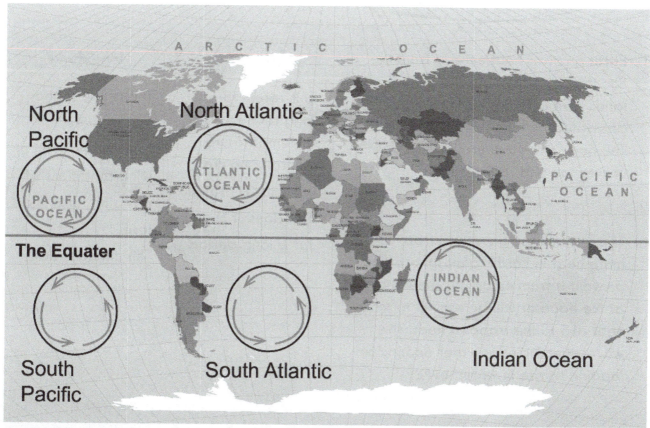

3. Surface ocean currents and Deep ocean currents

4. Surface ocean currents are driven by winds. The surface ocean currents at the equator are driven to move away from the equator due to the rotation of Earth. The currents above and below the equator circle away from the equator. This is a natural phenomenon called the Coriolis effect.
The deep ocean currents on the other hand are driven by differences in saltiness and temperature of the water. These are also called Thermohaline currents.

Greenhouse Effect

1. Earth receives heat energy from the Sun through radiation. The oceans and lands give out heat and this heat is dissipated through radiation as well. The Earth's atmosphere is heated up by convection and radiation.

2.
a. The greenhouse gases will trap more heat in Earth's atmosphere and prevent it from escaping. The water at the equator will be subject to more heat due to this trapped heat. This will further increase water expansion leading to rise in water level.

b. i. The water risen due to expansion will be driven toward the north and south poles thereby driving more surface currents.
ii. More warmer currents at the poles will cause melting of icebergs at poles thereby slowly causing a rise in water levels.
iii. Heat trapped in the Earth's atmosphere, over time, will cause an increase in overall global temperature, thereby causing global warming.

Climate vs Weather

1.

Climate	Weather
This refers to a long term record of temperature, rainfall/snowfall, wind for a region. This doesn't change for a long period.	This refers to the temperature, rainfall/snowfall or wind conditions of a region for a short term. This changes daily.

2.

Name of the state	Weather Conditions	Climatic Conditions
Texas	The temperature on 26th July 2019 was 90°F with wind blowing at 15 mph. On Christmas day, 2019 the temperature was 18°C during the day and 6°C during the night.	Summer in Texas lasts from June to August with a temperature ranging between 86°F and 98°F. Winter lasts from December to February with a temperature ranging between 45°F and 65°F.

Name of the state	Weather Conditions	Climatic Conditions
Arizona	Hawley Lake in Arizona recorded the coldest temperature of -40°C on January 7, 1971.	Winter lasts from December January in Arizona where January is the coldest month. Night temperatures are below freezing in northern and central parts but are mild in the south and west.

Name of the state	Weather Conditions	Climatic Conditions
New Jersey	New Jersey recorded a humidity of 86% and temperature of 11°C on 9th April 2020.	The hottest months in New Jersey are from June to August with temperatures ranging from 77°F to 87°F. The temperature in winter ranges from 49.2°F to 38°F.

Name of the state	Weather Conditions	Climatic Conditions
Illinois	The wind blew at a speed of 21 mph on 8th April 2020 and recorded a temperature of 6°C at 10 am.	Autumn in Illinois is from mid October to November with average day temperature ranging from 15.6°C to 21.1°C and night temperature ranging from 4.4°C to 10°C.

Physical Sciences

Heat Energy and Heat Transfer

Heat Transfer

a. Conduction

b. Radiation

c. Convection

Testing Heat Transfer

Sample answers:

- The hob gets heated.
- Heat from the hob heats the air closer to it.
- Hot air becomes lighter and rises to reach the hand.
- Hand feels warm.
- Since there is no contact between the heat source and the hand and there is no liquid here, the method of heat transfer here is by radiation.

Heat Transfer

- Heat from the kettle gets transferred to the water in it by convection.
- Heat from the hot water in the vessel gets transferred to the glass by conduction.
- Heat moves from warmer regions to cooler regions.

Heat Transfer Through Materials

- Metals are the best suited for saucepans as they conduct heat energy better than wood or plastic. Wood does not conduct heat. Plastic gets deformed and melts when subjected to heat from a stove.

- The method by which heat is transferred from the saucepan to the food in the pan is by conduction. Solids food contents get cooked by conduction of heat. The heat from the solid saucepan gets in contact with the solid food contents, thereby cooking. Liquid food such as soups get cooked by convection. The heated liquid closer to the heat source becomes less dense and rises while the cooler liquid on top sinks down to get heated.

Modes of Heat Transfer

1. Convection
   Heat transfer through motion of gases and liquids.

2. Conduction
   Heat transfer through motion of atoms and molecules and happens only through contact.

3. Radiation
   Heat transfers through energy waves without any contact or movement of atoms/molecules.

Life Sciences - Ecology

Energy Flow in Living Things

Ecosystem and its Factors

1. Living things - Fish (big and small), turtles, frogs, bugs, dragonfly, racoon, deer, hawk, plants,
   Nonliving things - sunlight, air, water

2. Producers - Plants/grass/cattail/water lily/water plants Consumers - Fish (big and small), turtles, frogs, bugs, dragonfly, racoon, deer, hawk
   Food chain sample :
   cattail → dragonfly → fish or frog → racoon or hawk

3. Plants will stop making food and eventually die out. Animals dependent on these plants for food such as deer, racoon will be left with no food. They will either move to other places in search of food or die out.

4. The pond will dry out eventually. Plants and animals dependent on the pond water will die out eventually. Animals dependent on the animals in the pond for food will be left with no food.

5. The number of frogs will reduce. The number of insects that feed on the plants will increase and end up eating more plants. This will reduce the food for herbivores.

6. It will affect the water plants, plants on the banks, animals in the ponds which might die out. Animals feeding on the pond animals might die out due to poisoning.

Producers and Consumers

Producers	Consumers
Flowers	Bees
Seeds	Birds
Greens	Hannah

Food Chains and Food Webs

1. Three

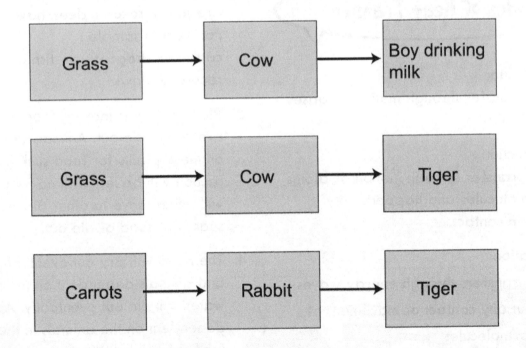

2. Different food chains link together to form a food web.

3. Yes

4.

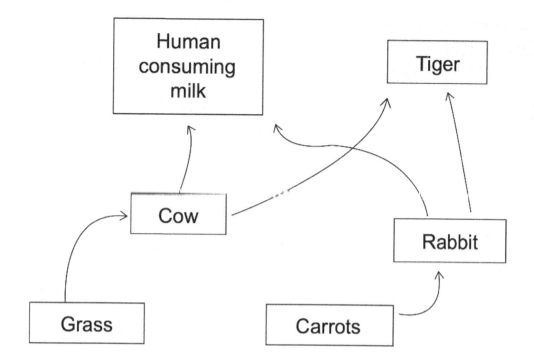

5. Herbivore: Cow, Rabbit
   Carnivore: Tiger
   Omnivore: Human

Energy Flow in Food Webs

1. Maize plant → Insect → Frog → snake → Hawk

2.

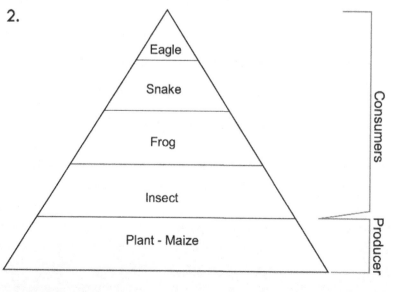

In an ecosystem there are more producers than consumers. When a herbivore, such as the insect in the food chain above consumes the plants, not all energy of the plant is passed on to it. Some energy is lost as heat or waste. The frog that consumes the insect does not get all the energy. This continues until the Eagle. As the shape of the pyramid suggests, the energy at the bottom is the maximum with producers and least at the top with the final consumer.

Relationships between Organisms

1. There are about 9 possible answers. Sample answers are:

   a. Corn → grasshopper → frog → python → eagle

   b. Flowering plant → butterfly → dragonfly → thrush → eagle

   c. Flowering plant → butterfly → frog → python → eagle

   d. Lavender → butterfly → frog → snake → eagle

   e. Mangoes → fruit fly → dragonfly → thrush → wolf → python → eagle

2. (Any three) Producers - mangoes, lavenders, flowering plants, corn
   (Any five) Consumers - grasshopper, frog, butterfly, dragonfly, wolf, python, eagle, thrush, fruit fly

3. Producers obtain their energy from the Sun.

4.
   a. Predator/Prey & Competition

   b. Predatory/Prey

   c. Predator/Prey

5. Competition: Frog and thrush, Wolf and eagle
   Predator/Prey: grasshopper and frog, frog and python, fruit fly and dragonfly

6. Eagle will be placed on top of the pyramid and the plants at the bottom. In an ecosystem, the producers are the maximum and the consumers are far less in number than the producers. Also, the energy from the producers is not completely transferred to the consumers. As we go up the food web, we can observe that an eagle's food and energy requirements depend on the energy of so many other animals. Energy transferred between these animals diminishes as it goes up the web/pyramid.

Animals and Adaptations

Reason behind Adaptations

1. The Tundra region is extremely cold and the world's coldest region. It is treeless. The monkey must develop a furry coat to protect itself from extreme cold conditions. It must also adapt to feed on woody shrubs as there would be no trees.

2. The fennec fox must develop swift moving skills and ability to climb trees. This is because the tropical rainforests are filled with trees and animals like the jaguar, leopard which are swift and move on trees as well.

Who am I?

1. Koala
2. Cobra
3. Elephant
4. Yak
5. Anteater
6. Kangaroo rat
7. Sea lion

Resources

Types of Resources

Renewable and Non-Renewable Resources

1. Petroleum, Non-renewable
2. Wood, non-renewable
3. Burning coal, non-renewable
4. Wind, renewable
5. Water, renewable

Compare and Contrast

Renewable Resources	Common Attributes	Non Renewable Resources
Wind Water Sunlight Can be replenished Do not cause pollution	Energy resource Can produce electricity	Fossil fuels Wood Natural gas Cannot be replenished Oil Cause pollution Coal

www.prepaze.com

1. A renewable energy source that is available in plenty and allows us to breathe is wind.

2. A resource that can be replenished is said to be renewable.

3. A resource that cannot be replenished is said to be nonrenewable.

4. The energy resource that is formed over millions of years and cannot be replenished is fossil fuels.

5. The resource used to burn and obtain electricity is coal.

6. Uranium is used in the making of nuclear energy.

7. Wood or corn make the biomass from which fuels are made.

8. Petroleum is another name for oil.

9. A nonrenewable resource which is pumped out from pockets both onshore and offshore is natural gas.

10. Solar energy is obtained from the Sun.

e	u	b	n	i	x	i	o	i	r	q	f	d
r	n	p	o	m	c	j	l	u	g	p	o	v
t	h	e	n	u	c	l	e	a	r	k	s	s
c	v	t	r	m	n	m	a	y	h	c	s	a
y	g	r	e	n	e	r	a	l	o	s	i	g
b	r	o	n	n	a	n	d	s	i	i	l	l
j	n	l	e	e	d	b	f	s	i	h	f	a
k	i	e	w	o	f	j	i	a	o	g	u	r
h	q	u	a	r	g	d	j	m	l	f	e	u
y	w	m	b	t	s	n	c	o	a	l	l	t
r	e	n	l	p	a	i	k	i	z	s	s	a
i	k	r	e	n	e	w	a	b	l	e	o	n

www.prepaze.com

Biomes That We Live In

1 and 2. Heating electrical appliances, cooking appliances, washing and drying appliances

3. High

4.

a. Renewable

As renewable resources can be replenished in a short period of time and will be less polluting.

b. Any renewable resource - solar energy, electricity obtained from hydroelectric power

c. Solar energy - March to august as it is sunny and maximum energy can be obtained.

Vocabulary Check

1. natural resources
2. contribution
3. conservation
4. nonrenewable
5. global warming
6. solution
7. sustainable
8. recycle
9. fossil fuels
10. solar energy
11. reuse
12. climate change
13. pollution
14. greenhouse gas
15. renewable

www.aceacademicpublishing.com

THE ONE BIG BOOK

GRADE 6

For English, Math, and Science

Ace Academic Publishing
ACHIEVING EXCELLENCE TOGETHER

Made in United States
Orlando, FL
15 August 2023